What people are saying about . . .

WisdomBuilt
Biblical Principles of Marriage

We had some very rocky times in our marriage. But because we watched Paul & Linda live a Godly, Christian marriage, we gratefully accepted their counsel and it saved our marriage. We are blessed to have known and stayed friends with them.

Sig & Becky Fertig, Church Members, Board of Deacons, Lay Ministry Leaders

I highly recommend WisdomBuilt Biblical Principles of Marriage. This practical and readable volume will enrich and strengthen marriage relationships. What makes this such a relevant book is the way Paul integrates insights from current research and the best of psychological studies—underscoring the reality that "all truth is God's truth." This will be valuable for any couple to read and study together as they strive for a healthy relationship. And, for church leaders wanting a great small group resource to enhance the marriages in their congregations, this book is a winner!

Rich Guerra, Superintendent, SoCal Network, Assemblies of God

In plain, storytelling fashion, Paul provides a simple, but not simplistic, application of timeless Biblical principles to apply in your relationship. He shares his own experiences of struggle and triumph, letting you know none of this is easy, but it is accessible. Paul's style is enjoyable, easy to read, and digest. I really appreciate his Discussion Starters at the end of each chapter to guide a couple's deeper dive. As a Christian couple's therapist, I highly recommend this to those who are contemplating marriage, are early in their marriage, or may be looking for ways to grow in their marriage.

Rick Hendricks, LMFC, Deputy District Director
North Atlantic District 1, Veterans Health Administration

Dr. Linzey offers a fresh perspective about the power of scripture as it pertains to married life, and practical solutions to common marital challenges. He will have you thinking one minute and laughing the next. Definitely on my list of books to recommend to couples I counsel. Couples need biblical wisdom in order to successfully navigate the changes of life and the storms they will encounter along the way.

Dr. Paul J. Kramer, LMFT
President, Remarkable Marriage & Family Institute

I have had the privilege of knowing Paul Linzey for several years. He brings his knowledge of the Bible and skill as a writer to his years of experience as a Pastor and Army Chaplain, and creates WisdomBuilt, a book on the Biblical Principles of Marriage. This is a must read for any couple preparing for marriage and a resource for those couples who are looking to strengthen their relationship.

Colonel Rob Noland, US Army Chaplain, Retired

I recommend WisdomBuilt Biblical Principles of Marriage without hesitation, and am grateful to have a copy for use in assisting couples in staying together and staying happy. I often work with marriages in deep distress. Many resources offer help, but are theoretical or "ivory tower" perspectives that lack the valuable element of Biblical Truth and proven experience. WisdomBuilt is a superior resource for couples. Dr. Linzey builds a solid foundation from Scripture, then adds constructive material which offers wisdom for building a strong and healthy marriage, a lasting relationship, and answers for marital problems. He and his wife, Linda, use their experiences and prayer-saturated victories to provide principles for building a marriage that will last a lifetime. They offer Godly wisdom which will help any couple renew their love, revive respect, and maintain a strong relationship. I am confident this book will be extremely helpful. Dr. Linzey has my blessing to offer himself and his material to our pastors and congregations.

Terry Raburn, Superintendent,
Peninsular Florida District, Assemblies of God

I love the approach Dr. Linzey takes in this book. Pastors need truthful, concise, meaningful materials to use in pre-marital and marital counseling. I've had a hard time finding that, and I've searched. Most marriage material is too complicated. I find that this material will make my job easier due to the variety of topics and the way they are laid out. *WisdomBuilt Biblical Principles of Marriage* should be a part of a required class in pastoral ministries. It could also be used to train pastors at the sectional or regional level. It is helpful, practical and useful. I have already used some of this material in a sermon and it was very well received.

T.J. Roberts, Lead Pastor, Venture Church, Lochbuie, CO

Engaging . . . enlightening . . . readable . . . wise. These are part of the avalanche of thoughts emerging from this fresh look at marriage. The subject matter ranges from the nitty-gritty of life, such as how to have a good fight over who takes out the garbage, to the ecstasy of marriage. I didn't realize, for example, that "backgammon" could be a code-word for sex. The chapter on embracing the image of God in the other is itself worth a read of the full text. Here, Paul Linzey emphasizes that valuing one's spouse reflects our valuing of God and that our valuing of God should extend into the valuing of our spouse as ourselves.

Dr. Zach Tackett, Professor of Historical Theology & Worship
Southeastern University

Paul brings honesty, passion, and humor to all he does, and this book is no exception. Readers will be blessed and encouraged by his ability to communicate biblical foundations and God's desire for a loving and lasting marriage.

Rev. Kathy Hulin, Director of Family Ministries
All Saints' Episcopal Church, Lakeland, FL

WisdomBuilt
Biblical Principles of Marriage
Second edition

Paul Linzey

P & L Publishing
& Literary Services

WisdomBuilt Biblical Principles of Marriage

Second edition

Copyright © 2021 Paul Linzey
ISBN:

Cover photo from pixabay.com

All rights reserved. Except for brief excerpts for review purposes, no part of this book may be reproduced or used in any form without written permission from the author.

Many of the names have been changed to protect the privacy of the people in the stories.

Unless otherwise noted, all Scripture quotations are taken from the HCSB®, Copyright © 1999, 2000, 2002, 2003, 2009 by Holman Bible Publishers. Used by permission. HCSB® is a federally registered trademark of Holman Bible Publishers

WidsomBuilt® is the mentoring ministry of Dr. Paul Linzey.
paulinzey.com

P & L Publishing
& Literary Services

plpubandlit.com

DEDICATION

To the many couples who used these principles
to build and maintain a positive, happy relationship
that stands the test of time.

To Linda:
Wife, ministry partner, and best friend.
Thank you for living these principles with me.

To Chris, Kevin, and Jeff:
Three sons who have provided friendship,
inspiration, and camaraderie your entire lives.

Being in relationship with my family has made me a better person,
forced me to evaluate my attitudes, and led me to search the
scriptures. Because of you, this book is possible.

CONTENTS

Acknowledgments	x
Preface	xiii
Foundational Beliefs	xix
1. Sidekicks	3
2. Baggage	17
3. On the Same Team	31
4. Heaven on Earth	45
5. Sex & Sensuality	55
6. Are We Having Fun Yet?	69
7. You've Got a Friend in Me	79
8. Yada, Yada, Yada	91
9. Now You're Talkin'	103
10. Title Deed	121
11. Give and Take	133
12. Imago Dei	147
Atmosphere/Climate	157
If You Want More	163
New Testament One-Anothers	165
Biblical Principles of Marriage	167
Bibliography	169

ACKNOWLEDGMENTS

The longer I'm married, the more I study the Bible, and the further I read the research of counselors and psychologists, the deeper I realize there is a remarkable amount of wisdom to be gained from each source. What's even more impressive is the extent to which they agree with each other. The more I train in ways to help people, the greater awareness I have that the Bible already speaks to those issues. It's from a commitment to the authority of the Word of God that I present these *WisdomBuilt Biblical Principles of Marriage*.

I am indebted to many clinical researchers, counselors, writers, biblical scholars, professors, pastors, lay leaders, and chaplains who sacrificially give of themselves to help couples improve their marriages. I would not be nearly as effective without their work. In addition, I am grateful to many personal friends in these fields who have made a difference in my life. They helped me personally as well as professionally.

There are many others who informed my thinking and helped shape the fascinating, practical ways of serving people in the U.S. Army, the Church, and the community. I am grateful for their impact on my life. My dear friends, Sig and Becky Fertig, Paul Kramer, Rob Noland, Rick Hendricks, Terry Raburn, Zach Tackett, Kathy Hulin, and Rich Guerra believed in me and gladly offered their endorsement. Chris Linzey offered some timely suggestions for the cover image and design. I am grateful for the many couples and individuals who shared their lives and their stories.

Dr. Linda Linzey, my wife and personal editor, was a remarkable asset in all aspects of discovering these principles, living them day by day, teaching them in church, military, and seminar settings, and putting them into book form.

John Donne wrote, "No man is an Island," and that is certainly true when it comes to completing a book like this one. I am but a "piece of the continent." Thanks to all of you for your friendship and encouragement.

PREFACE

A house is built by wisdom, and it is established by understanding; by knowledge the rooms are filled with every precious and beautiful treasure.

Proverbs 24:3-4

Falling in love is a wonderful experience. You're on top of the world, and you feel like you're the luckiest person in the world, hoping it'll last forever. Then it starts to change. At first it just doesn't feel the same. Then comes the pain, followed by the realization that it's over. Soon, you're singing the oldie from the Carpenters, *Goodbye to Love*.

Too many marriages in the United States end in divorce, and many of those who stay together aren't happy. The burning question is this. What are you and your spouse going to do to make sure you stay together and are happy?

After we'd been married five years, my wife and I came to a point where life was hard. We didn't have enough money to pay the bills. Linda was stuck at home with a toddler and an infant. She noticed that I invested a lot more time, energy, and thought in my work than I gave to our marriage. We were both dissatisfied and unhappy. We weren't getting enough sleep. Stress was high. We got angry easily, and didn't laugh much. We also discovered that men and women speak different languages. She was too emotional, and I was too insensitive.

One day, I came home from work and Linda met me in the kitchen. Without hesitation, she blurted out, "Are we ever going to be happy again? Will our marriage ever be good again?" I told her, "I think so, sweetheart. I'm not sure, but I think so."

It would have been easy to throw in the towel and call it quits. Just as easy to start blaming, accusing, and getting angry with each other. Or maybe even look elsewhere for love and affection, and have an affair. But we didn't do that. Instead, we decided to do our best to be kind to each other, treat each other right, and see what happened. Eventually, the joy did return. We got through that dark time, and we're glad we did. But we needed to help each other through the process.

Experts researching the biology and chemistry of falling in love and falling out of love have discovered there is a 2-year cycle of attraction, that is largely hormonal and chemical. What we call *falling in love* is the rush of hormones and chemicals that bring an excitement, arousal, happiness, and energy. You feel so good when you're with the new lover, or even when thinking about him or her. It's intoxicating.

Then after about two years, that chemical/hormonal cocktail begins to lose its effect. You don't feel the same, and you wonder what went wrong in the relationship, why you fell out of love. George Strait recorded a song titled *I Ain't Her Cowboy Anymore*, about a guy whose lover is leaving, and he has no clue what he did wrong . . . or whether he did anything wrong at all.

The answer? Nothing went wrong. There's a normal cycle that's part of developing a mature relationship. Yes, it's ignited by the passion and the internal chemistry, but then you have to build your marriage on a solid foundation so when the newness wears off, you don't fall into the trap of thinking, "Oh we're not in love anymore. It's just not meant to be. Maybe I married the wrong person." The plan is to fall madly in love, and then take the time and the effort to install the relationship values, skills, and patterns that'll take you through every phase of married life . . . Happy and together.

Let's simplify things here. There are two goals in marriage: stay together, and stay happy. Easy to say; tough to do. You need wisdom if you want to reach those goals. Proverbs 24:3-4 says, *A house is built by wisdom, and it is established by understanding; by knowledge the rooms are filled with every precious and beautiful treasure*, and these verses provide a starting point for this book.

When the proverb uses the word *house* or *home*, it's really talking about the people and the relationships in the home. *A house is built by wisdom,* means developing a great relationship requires wisdom. And filling its rooms *with every precious and beautiful treasure* is what every couple, family, and household should be trying to do.

WisdomBuilt will show you how to build your house in such a way that you discover the beauty, the grandeur, and the immeasurable treasures God has for you. In the same way every home is decorated differently, no two marriages will look and feel the same. Your relationship will be unique because you are one-of-a-kind, but the wisdom offered here will show you how to bring out the best in yourself, your partner, and your coupleness.

The longer I'm married, the more I study the Bible, and the further I read the research of counselors and psychologists, the deeper I realize there is a remarkable amount of wisdom to be gained from each source. What's even more amazing is the extent to which they agree with each other.

This book presents twelve principles for building a successful, joyful, fulfilling marriage, drawing from all three sources of wisdom. These principles have been in the Bible all along, but have often been misunderstood. Therefore, this book will be part Bible study, part counseling, and part storytelling.

The Bible, research, and personal experience come together to give couples the practical wisdom they need to grow a fantastic relationship, to offer congregational leaders a powerful resource for ministering to the couples and families in their care, and to provide correction for the wrong messages we often give people who are looking for help.

Several years ago, my wife and I bought a new house. We selected the floorplan, discussed the options we wanted, chose the property, and gathered all the documents needed for the financing. But, even with a lot of prayer and communication, we didn't agree on everything. Therefore, in order to end up with a home that we both liked and would be happy in, we had to work through the issues and take turns giving in. I had to be willing to say what really mattered to me, and Linda had to tell me what she felt strongly about. We spent hours and hours to get there, but it was worth the effort because we ended up with a house that is attractive, well-built, and meets our needs.

Once the papers were signed and the financing arranged, our house took several months to build. We made frequent visits to the property to see the progress, ooh-ing and ah-ing over every detail.

As you work together through these principles, you'll do the same thing. You'll talk, you'll discover new insights, you'll have disagreements. And you'll ooh and ah as you see growth in your marriage, your spouse, and yourself.

You're welcome to email me whenever you have a question. My website is paullinzey.com and the *Connect* page is a great way to reach me. If you're part of a congregation, you should also consider talking with your pastor, priest, or other ministry leader to get his or her input.

I understand that not everyone will agree with these principles. That's OK. What matters most is that you as a couple work together to build a home that is attractive, well-built, and meets your needs. If this book helps you do that, it will have accomplished its mission.

The concept of decorating your home *with every precious and beautiful treasure,* makes me ask, *What are the treasures it's talking about?* There are a lot of possibilities for what those treasures are; the proverb doesn't specify.

However, the Bible, clinical research, and personal experience indicate that there are at least four priceless treasures your home must have if you're to reach the two goals. If you have those treasures, you are light years ahead of most couples, and well on your way to a great life together.

The four treasures are Unity, Fulfillment, Insight, and Freedom. When these conditions are realized in your home and your marriage, you have the potential for maintaining a lifelong marriage, full of happiness and joy. Couples who don't have those qualities find just the opposite is true, because without them you are Divided, Empty, Clueless, and Trapped. As a couple, you need to decide whether you want your life experience to be:

- United or Divided
- Fulfilled or Empty
- Insight or Clueless
- Free or Trapped

If you decide you like Unity, Fulfillment, Insight, and Freedom more than their opposites, then this book is for you. The principles in each chapter add together to help you decorate your home with these treasures. When a couple lives these principles every day, that's what the result will be. You can count on it.

I hope you'll read this, and then take time as a couple to discuss the questions at the end of each chapter. You might want to form a class or a home group with a few other couples who are interested in building their marriages. And if you feel like it, you might consider asking your pastor to plan a marriage seminar or couple's retreat. Doing a seminar or retreat can be a lot of fun, and really helpful for the couples who participate.

As you're reading and discussing this material, you should ask yourself these questions: What are you going to do to make sure you're happy? How can you make sure you stay together? Is your foundation established and ready to build on?

FOUNDATIONAL BELIEFS

Therefore, everyone who hears these words of Mine and acts on them will be like a sensible man who built his house on the rock. The rain fell, the rivers rose, and the winds blew and pounded that house. Yet it didn't collapse, because its foundation was on the rock.

Matthew 7:24-25

In 2008, developers built some high-rise condos on the Southern Texas Coast. *Ocean Tower* was supposed to provide luxurious amenities and beautiful views, but it didn't take long for the entire structure to begin to sink, and then tilt, with wide cracks in the concrete support system. According to an old Turkish proverb, "A building without a foundation is soon demolished." The foundation wasn't prepared well enough, and the whole project had to be demolished after more than seventy-five million dollars had been invested.

The famous, leaning bell tower in Pisa, Italy, on the other hand, stood straight for five years before the 14,500-ton structure began to sink. It managed to survive, but as we all know, there is a serious slant.

In Matthew chapter seven, Jesus talks about the importance of a foundation for a home. But, just like in Proverbs 24:3-4, what he's really talking about is people, and in this case, the need for an inner, spiritual foundation.

Couples who want their marriage to survive the storms and shifting sands, need to make sure they have a foundation that will last a lifetime. *WisdomBuilt Biblical Principles of Marriage* provides that foundation. And these principles, themselves, are built on six foundational beliefs that serve as the basis for my work with couples.

1. There is a God, and he has revealed himself to people.
2. God made human beings, both male and female, in his likeness, the *Imago Dei*.
3. God designed marriage to be a picture of the love relationship he wants to have with people.
4. Marriage is the foundational relationship of the family and, therefore, the foundational relationship of society.
5. The Bible contains key principles which will help a couple develop a long-lasting, fulfilling, happy marriage.
6. God wants marriage to succeed.

Several years ago, my wife and I did a short-term missions trip to Budapest, Hungary, teaching a three-week intensive class at the Hungarian Bible college, and preaching at churches in and around the city. Our hosts were a missionary family that allowed us to stay in an upstairs bedroom in their home.

Looking out a second-story window, we noticed the neighbors were building another home on their property, immediately behind the main house. The missionaries explained that it was customary for children to grow up and live on the same property as their parents. The new building was for their son, who was about to get married. The foundation was already in place, and every day, we came back to the house, looked out the window, and followed the progress. We watched the walls grow higher as new rows of bricks were added.

That's the model used in this book The insight gained from the three sources of wisdom (the Bible, clinical research, and personal experience) will serve as your foundation. The twelve *Biblical Principles of Marriage* will be the bricks that you add to the walls of your house. Build them into your marriage, and you will discover the treasures that'll decorate your home, your marriage, and your life.

It's important to understand that all of the *Biblical Principles of Marriage* apply equally to both husband and wife. There aren't different sets of rules, as if men and women were from different planets. Remember, men and women are created in the Image of God. Both husband and wife are called to represent the Lord to one another.

Of course, there are personality differences, and there are definitely gender differences, just as there are family and cultural differences. But the principles apply equally. The goal is to understand the principles, and then figure out how to work them into your life, your marriage, your home, and your culture, letting the wisdom of the Word of God re-shape you, your values, and your behavior. In essence, the Spirit of God and the Word of God are working in your life, creating a new worldview and a new culture.

WisdomBuilt pulls these truths together, adds additional insight from clinical research and personal experience, and provides a biblical model for building and maintaining a good, strong marriage in which husband and wife are happy and fulfilled. The result is a practical, usable tool that may be used in your home or by leaders who want to disciple, mentor, or train the couples in their congregation.

God's plan for marriage is vastly different from the typical concept of marriage in the world today. Rather than a battle zone, marriage is designed to be peaceful. Rather than causing you pain, it can be a source of profound healing. Rather than a selfish coexistence, a good marriage is a loving couple coming together to help and encourage one another. Rather than a ball and chain, marriage liberates you to reach your goals and see your dreams come true. Rather than living in a kind of hell, marriage can be a heaven on earth. And, rather than a temporary arrangement, marriage is best when it takes you through all phases of life . . . together.

Let's get started. It's time to build a home that will last a lifetime.

TREASURE #1: UNITY

Jesus said whenever two come together in unity, he promises to be there with them. He followed that with another guarantee: whenever two are in agreement and ask for something, he will do it for them.

Do you catch the significance of this? Unity invites the presence of God and ignites the power of God. That's what makes unity a priceless commodity in your home. It's the single most-important component of an effective marriage.

The first treasure you need, then, to decorate your home is unity, and the *Biblical Principles of Marriage* will show you how to do that. When a couple puts these concepts into action in their home, they are able to create the dynamics that will sustain them and provide a deep awareness of the behaviors that contribute toward unity. They'll learn to avoid the words and behaviors that destroy unity.

When you are committed to building and maintaining unity in your marriage, you will experience the active presence of God and the awesome power of God. You'll start to decorate your home with this beautiful, priceless jewel, paving the way for more treasures to follow.

SIDEKICKS

Then the Lord God said, "It is not good for the man to be alone. I will make a helper as his complement.

Genesis 2:18

When I got home, Linda met me at the front door, placed both hands on my chest and said, "Stop right there, buster. When you come into this house, leave me and my kids alone."

I was speechless. Clueless might be appropriate, too. I didn't know what she was talking about. The only thing I could think to say was, "They're my kids, too."

But I totally missed her point, so she continued. "When you're gone, the boys and I are fine. We have a lot of fun. Life is good. But when you come home, you bring stress and anger, and you take it out on us: barking at me, criticizing the boys, grumping at everyone. Just leave us alone!"

Wake-up Call

Ouch! I had no idea I'd been doing that to my family. It never occurred to me that I was a problem. I decided it would be smart to do exactly what she said, so my new mission in life was to watch my family and learn from them. I didn't want my wife and sons to cringe when I came home. I didn't want them to think life was better when I'm gone. I wanted them to be glad I was her husband, glad I was their dad, and glad when I came home.

I made it my goal to make sure everything I said to my wife and sons was positive, and that my interaction in the marriage and the family was helpful. The confrontation at the front door that night changed me and the way I approached relationships. The Lord used Linda and her frustration to help me see a key biblical truth.

First Biblical Principle of Marriage: Designed to Help

The first time marriage is mentioned in the Bible, the word for Adam's new companion is not *wife, spouse,* or *partner*. God doesn't refer to Eve as Adam's *mate, lover,* or *better half*. He definitely doesn't call her *the old lady*. Not even *the missus*. No, the term God chose when he created marriage was "helper." Then the Lord God said, *"It is not good for the man to be alone. I will make a helper as his complement"* (Genesis 2:18).

Every time I read this, I start chuckling because this is the first time in the creation story God looks at what he made and doesn't say, "It's good." Instead, when he looks at the man, he says, "Hmmm. Something's not right here. He needs help."

You've probably heard the joke: God was practicing making people one day, and made a man. But after seeing the flaws and the mess he had made, he decided to try again. This time, he perfected his creation, made a bunch of improvements, and the result was a woman.

Or this one: God's original idea was to make only men. But after taking a look at the first one, God said, "No way this dude should be on his own. He needs help!" So, he added women to the plan, and the world became a better place.

Women have known for a long time, *Don't leave a man all by himself too long. That's not good.*

Sidekicks

OK, putting the jokes aside, at least we have to acknowledge that there's s a startling change in the pattern established in the creation narrative, because for the first time, God looks at what he made and doesn't say "It is good."

As we examine the scripture, we see that God himself presents a view of marriage that is theological, practical and visionary. Right from the start, the Lord makes it clear how he wants men and women to see each other, and how to relate to each other.

Marriage was designed for husband and wife to help each other. Why? Because life is hard, and we need help. We need someone who is there day after day, committed to making our life a bit better and more bearable. With a helper like that, life is more fun. There's more joy and satisfaction.

A lot of people think a helper is someone who is less important, less skilled, or less capable. Several dictionaries define a helper as an unskilled worker who is there to assist the tradesman or the professional. They offer synonyms like *assistant, adjunct, apprentice, deputy,* and *sidekick*. In our culture, a helper is considered *an underling, a hireling,* or a *subordinate*.

We call them *gophers*. We even talk about *the hired help*—people who do the tasks the important people don't want to do or don't have time to do. We see this in the novel, *The Help*, and the corresponding movie. It shows up in shows like *Downton Abbey*, too.

Famous Sidekicks

You can probably think of several characters in TV shows, comic books, movies, and novels who have a sidekick. There are lots of them: Sherlock Holmes and Dr. Watson, Batman and Robin, The Lone Ranger and Tonto, Han Solo and Chewbacca,

Don Quixote and Sancho Panza, Andy Griffith and Barney Fife, Captain Kirk and Spock, Robinson Crusoe and Friday, Robin Hood and Little John, Shrek and Donkey, Moses and Aaron, Paul and Silas.

It seems almost every hero has a sidekick who provides comic relief, but also offers serious friendship and assistance along the way. It's a classic technique in literature and drama, where sidekicks play an important role. They help the main character reach his goals or accomplish the mission. They offer friendship and provide insight. Usually, they perform tasks that are beneath the dignity of the hero. Sometimes they serve as a contrasting personality. The sidekick may be a commoner or a bumbler, allowing the audience someone they can relate with. Usually, the sidekick isn't quite as smart, but helps the star come up with brilliant ideas. Always, the sidekick is of lesser importance.

What Helper Really Means in the Bible

The problem is that we actually think the Bible supports the concept of a helper as someone who is inferior. No wonder we tend to think of the wife, and indeed, of women in general, as less important, inferior, and easy to make fun of or dismiss. But that's not what the Lord had in mind when he designed marriage, and that's not what helper means in the Bible.

The Hebrew word for a helper in the Old Testament is *ezer*, and comes from a verb that means to *rescue, deliver,* or *help*. Whenever it's used of human beings, it's talking about someone who is bigger, stronger, more powerful, smarter, or richer who reaches out to the weak or needy. Most often, however, the word *helper* refers to God himself. The psalmist wrote *God is my helper; the Lord is the sustainer of my life* (Proverbs 54:4).

Sidekicks

Some people think of a wife as the husband's sidekick. He's more important. He matters, and she doesn't. He makes the decisions. She's basically there to adorn his life and serve much like a classic sidekick. However, that's not even close to the meaning of helper in the Bible.

An example of help given by someone who is stronger, to one who is weaker is 2 Samuel 14:4, *When the woman from Tekoa came to the king, she fell with her face to the ground in homage and said, "Help me, my king!* The king was obviously richer, more powerful, and of greater worth in the eyes of the people. Yet, he becomes her helper.

It's astonishing that Genesis introduces woman this way, and that marriage is presented this way. In essence, the God who is our *Helper* created someone who will stand in for him and provide the help the man needs. It absolutely cannot be construed to refer to a lower-ranking female who helps the more-important male. God didn't make Eve to be Adam's sidekick.

No, God designed marriage to be a relationship in which husband and wife are devoted to helping one another. This is the first responsibility on their job description when they get married. God is our helper, and those who are married have a second helper. Someone they can rely on, trust, and gain strength from. Someone whose aim in the relationship is to contribute toward wholeness and happiness. Someone who lends a hand and provides help in a thousand little ways, and in some huge ways.

How Has Life Been Hard for You?

This is important because life is hard, and having a good helper can be a difference maker. Have you experienced any of these scenarios?

- There are tough decisions to make.

- As we age, our bodies fall apart. We get a serious illness, or lose some abilities.
- We carry the hurts from our past.
- Raising children is difficult.
- Finances are tough, and making ends meet is practically impossible.
- Loneliness is a terrible thing.
- Temptations are strong and destructive.
- We tend to drift and lose focus.
- We struggle with addictions or compulsive behaviors.
- People can be mean or unkind.
- Getting and keeping a good job seems impossible.
- Many people can't seem to find fulfillment or meaning.
- Life itself can be painful, which is why many consider suicide.
- A lot of us have been abused.

Talking with your partner about the struggles you've experienced can help you understand each other better and provide deep insight regarding your motives and actions. When you understand each other better, you're likely to fight less often and, instead, focus on ministering to each other and healing each other.

Help in the Bible

Helping is a major theme in the Bible. First, the Lord himself is our helper. Psalm 33:20 says, *We wait for Yahweh; He is our help and shield,* and in Psalm 46:1, *God is our refuge and strength, a helper who is always found in times of trouble.*

Second, the people of God are called to help others. Leviticus 25:35 says, *If your brother becomes destitute and cannot sustain himself among you, you are to support him as a foreigner or temporary resident, so that he can continue to live among you.* Ecclesiastes 4:9-10 teaches, *Two are better than one because they have a good reward for their efforts. For if either falls, his companion can lift him up; but pity the one who falls without another to lift him up.* In each of these scenarios, the helper is the stronger, richer, or more able person.

But the scriptural injunction to help others goes beyond the countryman, the friend, or the neighbor, extending even to one's enemy. Exodus 23:5, for example, says *If you see the donkey of someone who hates you lying helpless under its load, and you want to refrain from helping it, you must help with it.* And in Matthew 5:44, Jesus teaches his disciples, *But I tell you, love your enemies and pray for those who persecute you.*

A third way we see helping in the Bible is that ministry is considered to be a way of helping people. When describing Paul's Macedonian call, Acts 16:9 says, *During the night a vision appeared to Paul: A Macedonian man was standing and pleading with him, "Cross over to Macedonia and help us!"*

Fourth, there is a spiritual gift called the Gift of Helps in 1 Corinthians 12:28. *And God has placed these in the church: first apostles, second prophets, third teachers, next miracles, then gifts of healing, helping, managing, various kinds of languages.*

And fifth, marriage is initiated by God to be a helping relationship.

Husband and Wife: Designed to Help Each Other

If couples were to see their primary role in the marriage to be that of a helper, there would be some seriously helpful consequences. Instead of criticizing or attacking, they would try to determine how the partner might need help at this point in life, and try to provide that help. Sometimes the best approach is for a husband to simply ask his wife how she needs help, or for a wife to ask her husband.

One husband asked his wife this question and was stunned to hear her answer: "Well, for starters, you could stop making fun of me and talking bad about me to your friends." Another wife told her husband, "It would really help if you came home after work instead of playing sports every night of the week."

When a wife asked her husband the question, he replied, "I could use some help paying the bills. I've been really busy, and tend to put it off or forget." Another husband said, "I know I've been working a lot of hours lately, and it would really encourage me if you thanked me once in a while. Just to hear some gratitude would be a big help."

A person whose spouse is facing a particularly stressful time at work might offer to take a larger role in housekeeping and taking care of the children, whatever possible to help ease the burden, or perhaps see if the partner might like a massage, foot rub, or some other personal favor. Someone whose partner has recently experienced a setback or failure might want to be extra sensitive and aware of feelings, and might consider ways to build up and emphasize past successes and positive traits.

If the husband and wife both have jobs, perhaps they can help each other at home by sharing household chores such as cleaning, cooking, washing dishes, and taking the kids to their activities.

It's been said that marriage is a war in which two families send a representative to see which family will replicate itself. In other word, we tend to do things the way we experienced them in our family of origin, and we resist change.

When I was a kid, my mother was the one who took out the trash. When My wife was young, her father took out the trash. We came into the marriage assuming that the other would empty the trash every week, and it took us three years to realize nobody had emptied the trash. That last part is a joke, of course, but it underscores the fact that we had to work through our assumptions about household chores and how we can help each other in practical ways.

I came from a large family. My parents had ten children, and we all took turns washing and drying the dishes after dinner. In my wife's family, her mother always cleaned up after meals, so Linda assumed that she'd do the dishes when she got married . . . which was fine with me!

Thanksgiving Day Realization

It wasn't until after a Thanksgiving family get-together years later that I realized how hard my wife worked to plan, prepare, and serve the meal. And then more hard work to do all the clean-up and putting stuff away after the feast. So, I decided from then on, that if she prepared the meal, I would do the clean-up. I enlisted the aid of my sons and any other men who were with us for Thanksgiving. Amazingly, they all cooperated. My wife appreciated it, and I've continued the practice every day. It seems equitable, so I still do that.

Sharing the responsibilities in the home makes life better for both of us. I like vacuuming, mopping, and cleaning toilets. But I don't like cleaning tubs and showers. Linda volunteered to be the tub and shower cleaner. That's an act of love.

It's a good idea for couples to routinely take some time to check up on how they both might need help. This can be done while taking a walk, a picnic at a park, going out to dinner, or at home after the kids go to bed.

While driving home from work, you might start thinking about what you can do to be helpful when you walk into the house. Or, when an argument is building, husband and wife could ask themselves, "Is what I am about to say helpful?"

Lee Child, author of the Jack Reacher novels, tells about a time when he was unemployed. While trying to begin his writing career, he got into the habit of helping his wife with chores around the house. Then, he started going to the supermarket with her to help carry the groceries. She liked this, because he was quite a bit taller, able to reach items on the top shelves. On one occasion, a little old lady asked for his help. After Lee helped the woman, his wife said, "If this writing thing doesn't work out, you can always be a reacher in a supermarket." Instantly he thought, "What a great name for my character." And Jack Reacher was born.

The irony is that he was helping her in the supermarket, and she helped him by giving him a name for his character.

Having a proper understanding of the teaching on "help" in the Bible, couples who want their marriage to last a lifetime become extremely practical and intentional about helping their spouse in both small ways and big ways. They get good at it.

Christian psychologist Gary Smalley said helping is a powerful way of loving, empowering the partner to overcome the disasters that happen to everyone. According to Smalley, an "interest in being with and helping others during a crisis is a demonstration of love." Helping during the tough times can make or break a marriage, but having a helpful attitude and demeanor in the give and take of ordinary life is also essential.

Norman Wright and Gary Oliver point out that most couples begin their marriage responding to their partner's needs by going out of their way to meet those needs. "But in time, this changes. Where previously most of our attention was focused on our spouse's needs, our attention begins to focus on the fulfillment of our own needs. Each of us moves into the stage of giving less and expecting more." A relationship that began good, turns into disillusionment, and disillusionment invites what John Gottman calls the *Four Horsemen of the Apocalypse*: criticism, contempt, defensiveness, and stonewalling.

Dr. Gottman explains that once these behaviors are in the mix, the relationship is headed in the wrong direction, and may be in serious trouble. These actions simply don't help the situation, nor do they help the people involved. Talking seems useless. Husband and wife start living parallel lives. And loneliness sets in. Couples in a marriage where this is happening might feel like calling it quits. After all, that's what their friends, their families, their therapist, and the media are telling them to do. *You fell in love, it didn't work out, you fell out of love. Get over it, and move on.*

Throwing in the towel, however, might not be the best thing to do. That might just add more pain and failure to lives already in trouble. Instead, the wise couple will look for ways to help each other through the tough times. And, they'll look for responses that will help the marriage itself.

Marriage isn't a partnership where one is always weak and the other always strong. Everyone has strengths and weaknesses. The idea is to help each other maximize strengths, and overcome weaknesses.

Your Primary Role in the Marriage

When couples begin to understand that the primary role in marriage is to be a helper, they realize in a very real way that they represent God to each other. The Lord is our helper, and he places husband and wife in the marriage to act on his behalf.

The bottom line is that a husband and wife who will routinely help one another in practical ways day after day will establish a friendship and an atmosphere of love that is contagious, and noticeable to everyone who knows them. They're on their way to creating unity and developing a marriage that will last a lifetime.

Discussion Starters

 Key Concept: Your first and most-important role in marriage is to help your partner. This is just as true for a husband as it is for a wife.

 Discussion Points:

1. How has life been hard for you? For your partner?
2. Have you experienced God's help in any way?
3. Do you have a favorite sidekick in the movies or literature? Have you ever felt like you were a sidekick in your marriage?
4. If you and your spouse were to see yourselves as helpers in the relationship and consistently helped each other, what would be the consequences?

 **Dig Deeper:**

1. How has your partner helped you in the past? Have you said "thank you"?
2. In what ways might you provide the help your partner needs at this point in his or her life?

BAGGAGE

This is why a man leaves his father and mother and bonds with his wife, and they become one flesh.

Genesis 2:24:

Families have a powerful influence on you throughout your life. Parents, siblings, and extended family shape you, teach you, and help establish your values and worldview. A lot of people look like, sound like, and think like their parents, sometimes even the ways they laugh, sing, or walk. I read about some cities that have an annual father-son and mother-daughter look-alike contest, and the entries are fascinating. It takes just a few minutes on a computer to find some hilarious parent-child look-alikes.

What We Inherit

Personal interests, skills, and education often come from parents. It's pretty common for a child to grow up and go into the same line of work as mother or father. People tend to follow their parents' preferences in politics and religion, too. It makes sense, because parents set the tone in the home their children grow up in, and what the kids experience there, usually becomes the norm.

There's a short film about an interview with a Qantas Airline pilot whose son became a flier for the same airline. Steve Gist and his son, Taylor, eventually were assigned to fly together, with the dad as the lead pilot, and the son as the co-pilot. It's a great story, demonstrating some of the ways kids learn skills, knowledge, interests, and even careers from their parents.

I know of preachers' kids who become ministers, school teachers' kids who go into education, athletes' kids who play ball. The same happens with hobbies. In June 2011, two men (father and son) both scored their first-ever 300-point game at the same bowling alley during the same week.

When I was in high school, I played Lieutenant Joe Cable in the musical *South Pacific*. One of the songs was titled "You've Got to Be Carefully Taught." According to lyricist Oscar Hammerstein, we pick up hate and prejudice from our families.

We also learn how to behave in relationships from our families of origin, and that's what brings us to this principle. You see, most of us don't have very good role models when it comes to marriage. My wife and I both came from parents who had a pretty bad marriage, so when we got married, we didn't know what to do. We loved each other, but didn't know how to treat each other in positive ways, day after day.

Check Your Luggage

When talking about letting one's past influence the present, we often say the person is carrying some baggage. What we mean is, there's been some pain, abuse, or failure in the past, and the person hasn't finished dealing with it, letting go of it, healing from it, or forgiving the people involved. Whatever is in "the baggage" still has a negative impact on present-day relationships and attitudes.

Not all of the baggage we carry through life is painful or negative, though. In fact, sometimes it's the good stuff in our past that gets in the way of building a good marriage. People who come from a good family often have just as much difficulty forming a new marriage, because of the influence of the parents.

Second Biblical Principle of Marriage: Let Go of the Past

The second Biblical Principle of Marriage is found in Genesis 2:24: *This is why a man leaves his father and mother and bonds with his wife, and they become one flesh.* I call this verse the Old Testament equivalent of Philippians 3:13-14, *But one thing I do: Forgetting what is behind and reaching forward to what is ahead, I pursue as my goal the prize promised by God's heavenly call in Christ Jesus.*

The point of these scriptures is that in order to fully live in the present, you have to let go of the past. Spiritually, if you are to enjoy the Christian life and grow in the grace and knowledge of our Lord and Savior, you have to allow God's forgiveness to set you free from your sinful or destructive past, and move forward in a new direction, with different habits, forming a different lifestyle that is shaped by the Word of God and the Holy Spirit. This might require ending some relationships and forming new ones.

Relationally, if you want today's marriage to succeed, you have to stop focusing on previous relationships, good or bad. In order to be healthy and live in freedom today, you have to let go of the past in several crucial ways. A couple who want to have a fantastic marriage can't afford to live in the past

I have no doubt that my mother loved me, but she was a controller and manipulator who wanted to influence how my wife and I lived and how we raised our children. For example, Mom thought it was a sin to be left-handed. I had seen her take a toy or a spoon from a child's left hand and put it in the right hand.

Because my wife is a lefty, I knew there was a good chance that our children would be southpaws. So, when we were pregnant with our first son, I told my mother I didn't want her to remove a spoon, a crayon, or a toy from our son's left hand and put it in his right hand.

Mom yelled at me, "You can't tell me what to do, sonny-boy!"

"No, but if you ever do that, you'll not be welcome in my home, and you'll never see your grandson." As far as I know, Mom never did. And our son is left-handed.

During our early days of financial struggles, Mom offered to give us money, but always with strings attached, whether we would use it the way she wanted, or if we would make a decision she approved. It was tough for me to set boundaries, but my marriage needed it, and my wife appreciated it. We were better off without the money.

From what I've seen, that kind of control and manipulation is typical for a lot of families, and that's part of what has to be left behind when starting a new marriage. In fact, it's important for people from every family and every culture to take some time to think about how they should implement this principle, because it might look different from family to family and culture to culture.

Who's More Important to You?

One commentator discussing this principle believes the primary focus has to be a shift in loyalty. Before getting married, it's healthy and right to be loyal to one's parents and siblings. But once you get married, the primary loyalty has to shift to the new spouse.

It's not that you have to cut off relationship with your parents, brothers, and sisters. No, you still want them and need them in your life. But the spouse must become the new priority, and has to feel more important than the in-laws. To the extent you're willing and able to let go of prior loyalties, you can form new ones. Likewise, to the extent that you can't or won't change priorities, your marriage will suffer.

While the verse in Genesis states that it is the parents you must leave in order to form a new unity, there are others, as well. These might include a boyfriend, girlfriend, or a previous lover. In fact, there may be a number of people and situations included in what you let go of: friends, abuse, wealth, lifestyle, job, fame, high school sports, or any number of things in one's past.

Your Past Can Ruin Today

One couple lost a son in a terrible accident. Unable to let go of that pain and loss, not knowing how to heal, and unwilling to forgive, the woman drove her husband to divorce. She allowed the past to ruin their marriage by allowing it to remain in the present. She kept the pain alive.

But it's not just the negative that has to be left behind. Sometimes you have to let go of some positives: the good old days, a happy first marriage, that perfect job, a previous home and neighborhood, wealth or fame, or even a dream or ambition. An athlete whose playing days are over is often headed for emotional and relational disaster. A Soldier whose career comes to an end, sometimes can't adjust to being a civilian and finding a new identity.

Someone who loses a leg or an arm in an accident at work might have a tough time accepting the new reality and letting go of the previous physical ability. Retirees sometimes struggle with letting go of their previous life, identity, and sense of importance. Empty-nesters also face a difficult struggle when the kids are gone. These transitions are tough.

Sue Augustine writes, "All of us can think of something we'd like to be set free from. For some, it's hurtful memories, past regrets, or bitter resentment. For others it's sorrowful remorse, frightful insecurities, or deep-rooted grudges. Imagine what it would be like to be free . . . . There is hope for you or someone you know who struggles with an imperfect or painful past." Her book *When Your Past Is Hurting Your Present* is arranged in three sections: *Relinquish Your Past, Renew Your Present,* and *Rebuild Your Future.* This is good guidance for couples who are still fighting or struggling with letting go of the past.

Forgiveness is Powerful

It's crucial that you understand the power of forgiveness. When you forgive, you release yourselves from the pain and injustice in your past. But forgiveness doesn't happen quickly. According to Christian ethicist Lewis Smedes, it happens slowly, with a little understanding, and sometimes with some confusion, because it has to sort out the anger, the pain, and the injustice. When forgiveness has finished its work, however, both the forgiver and the offender have been renewed, transformed, and set free from the pain of the past.

Sometimes, you have to forgive the person you're still in relationship with because there's been unfaithfulness, a betrayal, neglect, or abuse. This is hard, but with God's help, and sometimes the help of a good pastor, counselor, or friend, you can be successful at putting the past behind you and moving forward in a fresh start.

Forgiveness doesn't mean there will be no scars. You carry the consequences of pain long after the hurting stops and the forgiveness is complete. The Christian singing group *Point of Grace* has a song that talks about the impact of the ugliness, pain, and shame of the past, which are often followed by scars that remain for a lifetime. *Heal the Wound,* written by Clint Lagerberg and

Nicole Nordeman, focuses on the metaphor that even after an injury has healed, there's often a scar that lasts a lifetime. But instead of seeing the scar as a negative, they reframe it as a reminder of how gracious the Lord was in bringing you through the struggle.

What Are You Hiding From?

In his book *Hiding from Love,* John Townsend says one of the hindrances to genuine intimacy is the pain and injury we received in the past. We keep hiding from love because the injury is still very real. Hiding, or avoiding intimacy, serves a useful purpose in an attempt to prevent further injury, but it can ruin your marriage.

Knowing about the hurts isn't enough, however. You have to do something about them. Dr. Townsend suggests finding safe relationships in which you can begin to heal the wounds from the past, taking responsibility for developing new relational skills, and letting go of your hiding patterns. In other words, if you do it right, and with people who are safe, you can give up your tendency to hide from love, in exchange for an authentic and healing relationship. This is what a good marriage accomplishes.

One middle-aged couple recognized they still carried some of the baggage from their past, so they decided to do something about it. They both had been in a previous marriage, and still felt some attachment and affection for their exes. In addition, there was guilt and pain because of some decisions they had made early in life. When they met with their pastor, asking for his guidance, he suggested that they create a private ritual, during which they would identify the aspects of their past they wanted to be free from. He also talked about how to forgive each other, and how to receive God's forgiveness.

They took a month to plan, and then went camping. The second day, they took a hike along a river, until they came to a suitable spot. They wrote down the specifics of what they wanted to let go of. After reading their lists to each other, they prayed and asked God to wash them, forgive them, and help them to let go of the past. They asked each other for forgiveness, too. Then, they threw their lists into the river. It was therapeutic to watch the pain of the past float downstream until out of sight. The river represented a washing or cleansing, and they were able to start fresh, committed to each other, committed to living in the present.

I'm not encouraging you to litter or throw trash into a river or stream. I'm merely telling you what they did. Another couple took their lists and burned them in a fireplace. Their baggage literally went up in smoke. You have to do what is meaningful for you, and what works for you.

To the degree that a couple is willing and able to leave the past, they have an opportunity to create a new unity as a couple. The opposite is also true. To the degree that you can't or won't let go of the past, you will be unable to create the unity essential to growing a healthy, happy marriage.

Different Kinds of Leaving

If Genesis says you're supposed to leave your parents, and Philippians tells you to let go of what's behind you, perhaps you need to talk about what that means. Depending on your family background, your personality, and the culture you come from, there seem to be several major categories of letting go of the past. These may include the following kinds of *leaving*:

- Residential: leaving your parents' home and moving into your own
- Emotional: leaving your parents emotional influence

- Financial: weaning yourself from financial dependence
- Identity: forming a new entity and identity with your spouse
- Authority: maturity includes no longer being under the authority of your parents

As hard as it is to do, the growing up process is designed to prepare you for effective, mature, adult life. This includes decision-making and participating in the world with a fully developed sense of responsibility. The parents' role is to bring their children to adulthood, and then turn them loose, allowing them to establish themselves, their new home, their new identity, and their new relationships.

On the other hand, you don't have to sever ties with everyone in your past. You want to be close with your parents, siblings, and friends for a lifetime. In a healthy family, and in relationships with well-adjusted friends, this can be done while developing a winning marriage. It's only when people in your past try to hold on too tight, influence too much, or demand too much, that they become a hindrance to your marriage. Anytime anything or anyone starts driving a wedge between you and your partner, you need to establish some boundaries and communicate them.

Every family has problem areas. We're all dysfunctional in some ways, even families that appear to have it all together. The art of growing up and maturing is to overcome your family's inherited dysfunction, and then pass on to your kids as few problems as possible.

We know one couple with five daughters. Every one of the girls was molested by the same uncle. Although their mother knew it was happening, she wouldn't do anything to stop her brother or protect her daughters. For some families, the problem is dishonesty. They're smart and talented, but most of the family members have a tendency to deceive. Another family might have deep-seated anger, or severe control issues.

Some dysfunctions are handed down from generation to generation, which means you can't overcome them on your own. You need each other's help. And you need the help of the Holy Spirit. It might require healing, forgiveness, and discipling or counseling if you're truly going to be free and form new patterns.

If you don't let go of the past, your baggage can haunt you the rest of your life. Similarly, past success can cause problems. If you continually compare them with today's failures, it's easy to become unhappy or bitter. You have to let go.

When there has been a betrayal of trust in your marriage, you have to be willing to end the betrayal, find a way to forgive, and put it behind you, or your marriage can't survive. The good news is that with God's help and with the help of your mate, you can.

Why Get Rid of Old Baggage?

Why is it important? Why do you need to let go of the past? First, health demands it. Those who can't let go and can't forgive might have all sorts of physical problems: stress, high blood pressure, heart disease, high cholesterol, inability to concentrate or focus, headaches, sexual dysfunction or disinterest, plus a variety of emotional and spiritual problems.

Second, unity depends on it. Anything that hinders unity in the marriage has to stop. If you're going to have a good marriage, and if you're going to experience the presence of God and the power of God, unity is a necessity. The people, the problems, and the pain of your past will always try to drive a wedge between you if you're not willing or able to put it behind you.

Third, your emotional and spiritual growth are determined by it. So, it's relevant to ask the questions: Do you want to grow?

Baggage

Do you want to be closer to the Lord? Do you want a closer, deeper, more fulfilling marriage? If your answer is yes, you have to let go of the past, focus on the present, and aim for the future …together. Then you'll be able to discover all that the Lord has in mind for you. The people, the problems, and the pain of the past will hinder you if not dealt with adequately. The key is not to get stuck there.

One woman told me that when she was a child, her grandfather frequently raped her. This abuse lasted several years, and the trauma ruined the first twenty years of her marriage. It wasn't until around age forty-five that, through a combination of counseling and spiritual guidance, she managed to break free from the control the abuse had on her. That's what it took for her and her husband to finally have the kind of marriage they wanted all along.

According to Lewis Smedes, there are four stages of the forgiveness process: We hurt. We hate. We heal. And then we forgive. His book *Forgive & Forget* is a powerful look at what it takes to forgive and let go of the past. The subtitle of his book is what it's really about: *Healing the Hurts We Don't Deserve*. Some people get stuck in the hurting and hating, and are never able to move beyond, like a sore that won't heal because you keep rubbing it, opening it up again.

If your marriage is struggling because of something in the past, you need to do something about it. There are some great books that can help. Seeing your pastor or counselor can make a huge difference. Pray and talk together as husband and wife. Don't let it ruin your marriage.

To the extent that husband and wife are able to let go of the past, you are able to build unity in your marriage. So, pack your bags. Say goodbye to the past. It's time to live in the moment, making the most of the opportunities you have right now.

Baggage

Discussion Starters

Key Concept: To the extent that husband and wife are able to leave the past, they are able to build unity, and form a successful, happy marriage.

Discussion Points:

1. What are some of the things you like about your family of origin?
2. Are there some people, hurts, or issues in your past that continue to influence you and your marriage in negative ways?
3. Has someone ever tried to drive a wedge between you and your spouse? Has it happened accidentally?

Dig Deeper:

1. When was the last time you had to ask your partner for forgiveness? When was the last time you forgave your mate? Is this easy or hard for you as a couple?
2. Talk with your lover and identify at least three goals for your future together.

ON THE SAME TEAM

This is why a man leaves his father and mother and bonds with his wife, and they become one flesh.

Genesis 2:24

Several years ago, my wife and I started using the expression, "We're on the same team" to emphasize the unity between us. During the fall season, we watch college football on Saturdays, and in the spring, *March Madness*, which is the end-of-season NCAA basketball tournament featuring the top teams in the nation. So, the team concept makes sense to us.

There might be a lot of players and coaches with different personalities and roles on the team, but there is a common goal that unites them . . . they win or lose together. Therefore, everyone in the organization focuses on teamwork, chemistry, and developing a team spirit.

You Win or Lose as a Team

Similarly, in marriage we have unique personalities and interests. We have different roles in the relationship, the family, and the household. But the bottom line is that we win or lose together. That's why we can't afford to fight against each other. It makes no sense to compete against each other. We are on the same team. If my wife succeeds, then I succeed. If I do well, she does well. Linda and I are very competitive when it comes to games, but we've learned that whether we win or lose at the backgammon table, the tennis court, or the card game, that isn't the issue. It's how we treat each other, because in real life, we're on the same team.

You don't cripple your partner, because the team needs him. You don't discourage your team member, because you need her to be at her best if the team is going to win. A team that implodes and fights against itself is a team in trouble.

During a basketball game, one player may inbound the ball by throwing it to a teammate. That partner dribbles towards the goal, then passes to a third member of the team, who is open under the basket and scores. The guy who makes the lay-up is credited with the score, but the one who passed him the ball gets an assist, after receiving the ball from the player who inbounded and got it all started. Some coaches have a policy that nobody tries to score until after the ball has been passed five times. He wants everyone on the team involved in the game every play, because they win or lose as a team.

Whether talking about the Super Bowl, the Stanley Cup, the Larry O'Brien Championship, or the World Series, after it's over and the champagne is spraying all over the winning team's locker room, a reporter inevitably asks the question of the coaches and players, "What is it about this team that made it possible to get to this celebration?" The answer is almost always the same. "There's a camaraderie on the field and off. We get along. We care about each other. We have a chemistry. We're a band of brothers, and it carries over to the way we play." They're talking about unity, and unity produces winners. The same is true for the NASCAR Monster Energy Cup and any other sport in the world.

Stay Focused

The team concept helps us stay focused on unity in our marriage, but each couple has to discover what works for them. For this reason, I suggest you and your spouse take some time to talk about unity, define it, and come up with a slogan, an analogy, or a word picture that summarizes the essence of what unity means for you. That way, you can develop a verbal shorthand to remind each other.

Life throws challenges, obstacles, and tough situations at you, and you simply can't afford to try to make your marriage work without the power of God switched on, or without the presence of God every single minute of every day. And yet, thousands of couples—even many Christian couples—don't seem to understand what's at stake.

Third Biblical Principle of Marriage: Created for Unity

The third *Biblical Principle of Marriage* comes from three scriptures. The first is Genesis 2:24: *This is why a man leaves his father and mother and bonds with his wife, and they become one flesh.* The first part of this verse contains the principle of letting go of the past. The second part introduces the concept of unity.

Another scripture is Matthew 12:25: *Every kingdom divided against itself is headed for destruction, and no city or house divided against itself will stand.* What do a kingdom, a city, and a marriage have in common? They can't exist long-term without unity.

It would be ludicrous for a king to attack his own realm. That would be a recipe for disaster. It would be absurd for a mayor or city council to intentionally harm the people of their city. No entity can last very long if there is internal division and strife. And, it would be a catastrophe for husband and wife to fight against each other. Yet, that's what's happening in too many homes. Yelling, insulting, slapping, and hitting have no place in your marriage. Name-calling, lying, betraying, and going behind your partner's back are always against the rules.

A third scripture is Matthew 18:19-20, which is the most explicit statement on the crucial dynamics of unity: *If two of you on earth agree about any matter that you pray for, it will be done for you by My Father in heaven. For where two or three are gathered together in My name, I am there among them.*

Most Important Principle for Relationships

The single most important principle concerning marriage in the Bible is unity, which is why this principle shares its name with Treasure #1. When God establishes a covenant relationship, it's an invitation to unity. That's why in John chapter 17, Jesus prays that his disciples may be one.

I pray not only for these, but also for those who believe in Me through their message. May they all be one, as You, Father, are in Me and I am in You. May they also be one in Us, so the world may believe You sent Me. . . . May they be made completely one.

In the same way the Father and the Son are in unity, the Lord wants his followers to be one. This is true for the collective Church, for individual believers, and also true for couples.

It's a continuation of the Old Testament theme of God dwelling among his people and of Matthew's earlier account of Immanuel, the God who is with us.

Jesus explains that where there is unity, the presence of God is invited in. And, where there is unity, the power of God is activated . . . automatically.

The problem is, the opposite is also true. Where unity is lacking, the power of God is unplugged or shut off, and the presence of the Lord is evicted . . . automatically. That's why unity is essential in our churches and in our homes.

The more I read the Bible, the more I understand that husband and wife were created for unity. Unity is what love is all about. Unity is what marriage is all about. Unity is what life is all about. Unity is what God is all about. When you as husband and wife focus on building and maintaining unity, you will create an amazing marriage. People will notice, and they'll ask, "What are you doing? What's your secret?" They'll want what you have.

How Would You Define Unity?

People define unity in many ways. For some it is being in agreement, while others talk about a feeling of harmony. Some describe it as getting along without fighting, while others say unity is a camaraderie. One aspect of unity is having a common purpose or cause, and some believe unity means being connected. How would you define it?

Willard Harley discusses the importance of unity in his book *His Needs, Her Needs*, and in *Effective Marriage Counseling*, which is a guide to using *His Needs, Her Needs*. Harley's sixth "Love Buster" is what he calls independent behavior, "activities that are conceived and executed by a spouse as if the other doesn't exist. It should be no surprise that spouses usually fight a lot when one ignores the interests and feelings of the other."

As an alternative to the independence promoted by popular culture, the media, and friends, Harley suggests a Policy of Joint Agreement (POJA): "Never do anything without an enthusiastic agreement between you and your spouse." Harley estimates that about eighty percent of American couples consider this rule to be ridiculous. No wonder they have a tough time staying together happy. Very few are living in unity.

Gary Chapman acknowledges that "one of the greatest problems in marriage is the decision-making process. Visions of democracy dance in the minds of many young couples, but when there are only two voting members, democracy often results in deadlock." He goes on to say that "the objective is always oneness in our decisions.... As imperfect beings, we may not always be able to attain the ideal, but that must always be our goal."

Chapman suggests that if couples are not able to come to agreement about a course of action, they should wait, and a few days later pick up the discussion again, still with the aim of agreeing on a decision. According to his research and experience, there are few decisions that have to be made today. "Most things can wait. Unity is more important that haste." In other words, a good decision at the expense of unity is a bad decision.

What It Comes Down To

The bottom line is this: anything that builds or promotes unity in the marriage is worth doing, and anything that destroys or hinders unity in the marriage should never be done. We have to be that practical about it, that pragmatic.

"Let's see. Should I insult my wife in front of her friends? Wait a sec. Would that build unity in our marriage? Oops. Better not."

"Should I buy that new dress, even though my husband has told me over and over that we don't have the money? Oh, that might hinder unity. Hmmm, OK, I won't."

"We agreed that because we've been too busy lately, we'd stay home this weekend and spend time together. But a friend offered me a ticket to the big game, and I really wanna go. I can't reach my wife on the phone, and I have to make the decision right now. What do I do? I guess I'll give the ticket to somebody else. I want to honor the agreement I made with my wife."

How Do You Get There?

There are several things a couple can do to achieve unity. First is to pray, asking God to bring unity to the marriage. James 4:2 says, *You do not have because you do not ask.* Prayer is an important part of maintaining unity in the home. Second is to put in the hard work. Do whatever builds or promotes unity, and don't do anything that destroys or hinders unity. Ephesians 4:3 instructs us diligently keep *the unity of the Spirit with the peace that binds us.* The context in Ephesians is the church, of course, but as Marriage Encounter has maintained for a long time, *a couple is the smallest church.* Couples who discipline themselves to think this way about unity have an advantage.

Third, control the tongue. Proverbs 18:21 says, *Life and death are in the power of the tongue.* With our words, we kill or heal the people in our lives. I've made the decision that I want to be a life-giving, healing influence for my wife and kids. Therefore, I try to choose my words carefully, especially when having a disagreement or an argument.

A fourth action is to honor one's agreements. A good relationship is always built on agreements. This is true whether we're talking about a business relationship, participation as a community volunteer, ministry in the church, or a marriage and family at home. According to Psalm 15:4, *the wise person is one who keeps his word whatever the cost.* He doesn't renege on an agreement, because he understands that an agreement is a commitment, and keeping agreements is what develops integrity.

Fifth is being kind to each other. Making the effort to do even small acts of kindness every day will add up. *Be kind and compassionate to one another,* Ephesians 4:32 urges us. Sixth, take time to think about each other. It's important to think about the spouse's qualities, strengths, and talents, and comment on them. Take time also to think about your spouse's needs, weaknesses, and interests, because caring about each other is an essential part of building unity.

And seventh, spend enough time together. Many couples are too busy. They think quality time compensates for not having enough time together, but it doesn't work that way. A couple seldom has *quality* time if there isn't *enough* time together.

Scott Stanley's research at the University of Denver indicates that couples who prioritize time together will continue growing in intimacy, friendship, and unity, whereas couples who are too busy will slip away from each other. "The problem we all face is that there is much less quality time when there is little quantity time. . . . That means you need to put some boundaries around all the other things you do in life, like the amount of time you devote to work, to carve out time for being together."

There are many behaviors that can hinder unity. These include yelling, screaming, cussing, insulting, attacking, hurting, accusing, blaming, having an affair, avoidance, busyness, and not keeping one's word. On the other hand, some of the actions that build or promote unity are keeping one's word, planning special times together, encouragement, faithfulness, paying attention to what's important to your spouse, helping in practical every-day ways, and helping in big ways.

The idea that a reluctant agreement is the same as unity, is deceptive and destructive. Trust me, they're not the same. If you're trying to persuade your spouse against his or her will, chances are you're not building unity. As Dr. Harvey's Policy of Joint Agreement says, "Never do anything without an enthusiastic agreement between you and your spouse." An *enthusiastic agreement* is not the same as a reluctant *Well, alright, but I don't like it.* The difference is huge.

But Is it Worth the Effort?

When a couple will do what it takes to build and maintain unity, the results are astounding.
- The presence and the power of God are at work in their life.
- Miracles begin to happen.
- They are healthier and happier.
- They can weather any storm and solve any problem.
- They win the battle against the kids, the neighbors, and the in-laws.
- They develop a great sex life.

The opposite is also true. A couple who doesn't maintain unity will undo the blessings just mentioned, and lose out on what the Lord has in mind for them. Interestingly, it's entirely up to you. Nobody else can make the decision for you. It's not up to chance, as if some people just get lucky and pick the right guy or the right gal, and it all works out. And, it's not up to just one of the persons in the marriage. It has to be decided and acted on together.

Unity invites the power and the presence of God into the home, and prevents the devil from getting a foothold in the most important of all human relationships. The wise couple will recognize this and do whatever it takes to promote unity, and stop doing anything that hinders it.

In Genesis 2:24 there's an understanding that unity is the most important factor in relationship. Two becoming one in marriage is essential for marital success and happiness. In

Matthew chapter 18, Jesus explains that where there is unity, the presence of God is invited in. And, where there is unity, the power of God is activated.

The problem is that the opposite is also true. Where unity is lacking, the power of God is unplugged, and the presence of the Lord is evicted. That's why unity is essential in your home. Unity produces winners, while division creates losers. Which do you prefer?

On the Same Team

Discussion Starters

 Key Concept: Unity invites the power and the presence of God into your home, and prevents the devil from getting a foothold in the most important relationship of all.

 Discussion Points:

1. Come up with a list of three or four activities that you and your partner like to do together.
2. How would you define or explain unity?
3. Share with your spouse something you do that might be hindering unity in your marriage. Identify a behavior your mate does that builds unity.
4. Now might be a good time to "count the cost" of working towards unity. What's it going to take? What behaviors, practices, or habits might have to change?

 **Dig Deeper:**

1. Which of the six results of unity listed in the bullet points on page 39 is most-needed in your home?
2. What agreements have you made with your mate? Are there some new agreements you should think about?
3. Take a few minutes to pray together. A simple, sincere prayer is OK. It doesn't have to sound fancy or theological.

TREASURE #2: FULFILLMENT

Each of the *Biblical Principles of Marriage* adds a dimension of fulfillment and a deep sense of satisfaction. According to Proverbs 3:5-6, the Lord will straighten the path and smooth the road for those who put these into practice. This is the same thought expressed in Isaiah 40:3-4, where the prophet talks about preparing the way for the Messiah. The crooked path shall be made straight. The lowlands shall be filled in, the mountains leveled, and the rough and bumpy ways made smooth. That's what the Lord wants to do in your marriage, and that's what husband and wife can do for each other.

Hebrews 13:4 teaches you to honor marriage in general, and to honor your marriage in particular. First Peter 3:7 adds that your prayers will be hindered if you don't honor each other.

The next three areas of fulfillment (Spirituality, Sexuality, Friendship) combine to bring an inner strength for you as an individual as well as for you as a couple. Your life can be pleasant, prosperous, and deeply satisfying when you get the wisdom contained in these principles. According to the scriptures, your prayers will be answered and your dreams will come true.

In other words, maybe you really can live happily ever after. Now that's a treasure worth adding to the décor of your home!

HEAVEN ON EARTH

Trust in the Lord with all your heart, and do not rely on your own understanding; think about Him in all your ways, and He will guide you on the right paths.

Proverbs 3:5-6

Couples who are active in their spiritual life together have a much higher rate of marital success. The opposite is also true. Couples who don't practice their faith together tend to fall apart when life gets tough or when there are sexual temptations. Pursuing faith together and maintaining a spiritual focus are crucial to growing a strong, close marriage.

For this reason, Kay Arthur teaches that your relationship with Christ is the glue that can bond a husband and wife together for life, the secret that can hold your marriage together.

Genesis 2:24 says when a man and a woman marry, *they become one flesh*. The emphasis is on physical intimacy or oneness. However, the unity the Lord wants couples to experience extends far beyond the physical dimension of the relationship. It includes intellectual and spiritual unity as well.

Humans are three-fold beings. We are physical, intellectual, and spiritual, and the Lord designed us to remain active in all three ways throughout our lives. To omit any one of these dimensions is to neglect a third of what life is all about. Some couples leave out two aspects of humanness in their marriage, focusing only on sex, disregarding the importance of the mind and the spirit. When they do this, they're limiting their relationship to only one-third of their potential for intimacy, meaning, and happiness together. They're simply too shallow as a couple, and their marriage is headed for troubled waters, certain to crash against the rocks or run aground.

Fourth Biblical Principle: The Gift of Spirituality

The fourth Biblical Principle of Marriage is found in Proverbs 3:5-6, which says, *Trust in the Lord with all your heart, and do not rely on your own understanding; think about Him in all your ways, and He will guide you on the right paths.* The wisdom found here encourages you to acknowledge the Lord in every part of your life.

This would include your career, your health, your finances, your lifestyle choices, and your relationships. It encompasses your education, the books you read, and the movies and shows you watch. And, it involves your marriage and family. In other words, if you want to know how to make your marriage work, it's important to start with making sure you are being spiritual together.

Close to the Lord = Close to Each Other

Early in our marriage, at a time when my wife and I were really busy, with three kids at home, finances that were really tight, and life was stressful, we didn't know the connection between spirituality and happiness in marriage. What we did know was that because of our circumstances, we got out of the habit of reading our Bibles, praying together, and taking time to worship together. We were totally unaware of the invisible toll it was taking.

We were snippy with each other, which isn't usually the case. We didn't have much patience. And, I was facing some strong sexual temptations. In the middle of this chapter of our lives, Linda said to me one day, "You know, we haven't prayed together or done family devotions in several weeks. I wonder if that's part of why we're struggling."

She was right. Almost as soon as we reinstated our spiritual disciplines, a sense of unity was restored, we got along better, and the other circumstances were much easier to handle.

A Gift from God

Spirituality, is a gift from God, designed to help us succeed in marriage, which is the most important human relationship. The Bible says *Every perfect gift is from above*. Spirituality is a gift designed by God to help us, to bring happiness and fulfillment, to draw us closer to him, and to one another as husband and wife. It's one of the ways God empowers us, helps us make sense of the world, and make sense of our lives.

The creators of the Prevention and Relationship Enhancement Program (PREP) at the University of Denver point out that spirituality is an important aspect of a successful marriage. They use the term "core beliefs," which can have positive and lasting effects on marriage. These core beliefs are the values, philosophies, spiritual ideals, culture, and worship practices that are fundamental to who you are as individuals and who you are as a couple. They definitely have a huge impact on your marriage.

According to PREP, there are two benefits of religion and spirituality: 1) having a social support group, and 2) sharing a worldview, with its accompanying core values. Couples need a support network that encourages faithfulness, loyalty, and problem solving, and shows them how to make marriage work.

They also need connections that help with depression, isolationism, and other problems. Many fellowships spontaneously offer transportation, childcare, or other services when there's a need. Religious congregations provide this kind of support.

Perhaps even more important than the social support aspect of being part of a religious group, however, is the power of sharing a worldview. When there is agreement on ideas, philosophy, spirituality, culture, and lifestyle, there's a powerful internal unity that empowers a couple to overcome the inevitable obstacles of life.

Dr. John Gottman's approach is that couples can create shared meaning. In his book *The Seven Principles for Making Marriage Work*, he says marriage is so much more than tasks and activities. It's not just about making love, having kids, and sharing household responsibilities. What's often missing, he says, is a deeper sense of shared meaning. This spiritual dimension is a vital aspect of human existence, and therefore, a crucial part of a meaningful relationship like marriage. Creating a shared inner life brings a couple together like nothing else ever could.

There Really is a God

More significant, however, is the fact that there really is a God who cares passionately about people, and makes his power available to you. Many couples have pursued spirituality by developing a personal faith in Jesus Christ, and have discovered that the presence of God and the power of God in their daily lives make an amazing difference for them.

In the introduction to his book *A Celebration of Sex*, Dr. Doug Rosenau mentions there are ten reasonable Biblical expectations which must be incorporated into a relationship for marriage to be at its best. Although I will refer to Rosenau's work in the next chapter on *Sex and Sensuality*, his list of reasonable Biblical expectations fits the discussion on spirituality also, so I will include it here. Many couples start out with a lot of incorrect, unhelpful, and unrealistic expectations, so Rosenau provides the following as a helpful corrective.

Rosenau's Reasonable Expectations in Christian Marriage

1. Each of us will have a best friend offering unconditional love, understanding, and support.
2. We can't meet all of each other's needs, or take sole responsibility for personal happiness.
3. We'll leave our fathers and mothers and create a new, independent, special family unit.
4. We'll have one healthy fight per week.
5. We'll take regular vacations and honeymoons.
6. We'll use credit carefully and become wise stewards of our finances.
7. We'll be faithful & committed to each other.
8. Either of us may initiate marriage counseling, and the other will gladly cooperate.
9. We'll have regular, satisfying sexual interaction.
10. We'll enjoy a growing spiritual life together, with prayer, worship, and Bible study.

Notice number ten in his list? Spirituality is a vital part of having fun, growing strong, and building a marriage that'll last forever. Too many people think they can simply cut out the spiritual aspect of life and still live a healthy, happy, normal life, but it doesn't work that way. We were created by God to worship him, to be in relationship with him, to enjoy him, and to develop spiritually.

Building a shared sense of meaning and values can have a profound effect on your marriage. You can have the presence and power of God working for you. You can be more in tune with God, yourself, and your mate. Your congregation can provide a healthy social support system. Bible study can help you grow, learn, and mature. Faith in God can reinforce healthy values and enhance a sense of unity in marriage.

God is Love

The reason for the connection between spirituality and closeness in marriage is because God is love. The closer we are to him, the more we are able to love the people in our lives. The more we understand the Lord and genuine spirituality, the more we can understand the importance of spiritual unity between husband and wife.

For many couples, sex is better when there is an intellectual and spiritual unity because the sharing of ideas adds depth and strength, and because God blesses those who draw near to him. To bless means to make happy, and happy people have a better chance to create and maintain healthy relationships because marriage is much more than physical oneness.

Jim George is an author/pastor who understands the importance of growing in the Lord, and the impact it has on your marriage. He opens his book, *A Husband After God's Own Heart*, with Matthew 6:33, *But seek first the kingdom of God and His righteousness, and all these things will be provided for you.*

According to George, putting the Kingdom of God first in your life has some powerful repercussions. It helps you determine your priorities, promotes purity, and leads to discernment: three qualities that go a long way to help establish a great marriage.

An important aspect of Christian marriage is the recognition that husband and wife are also brother and sister in the Lord. Therefore, all the verses in the New Testament that talk about how to treat one another in the Body of Christ, also apply to husband and wife. I refer to this as "One-Anothering." Marriage Encounter teaches that a Christian couple is the smallest church. After all, Jesus did say "where two are gathered I am there. And where two agree, I will do it." Therefore, it makes sense that a Christian couple should be spiritual together, and treat each other at least as well as the New Testament teaches all Christians to behave towards one another.

For example, I've seen couples who easily and quickly get angry at each other, yet the Bible says we should be slow to anger. Many couples hold grudges against each other for a long time, refusing to forgive, but the scripture teaches us to forgive each other and not hold wrongs against one another. Some couples are mean to each other, even though the apostle says we should be kind one to another.

It seems to me that a couple who wants to learn how to build a strong, happy, successful marriage should simply start with the New Testament One-Anothers, and put those into practice. You'll find a list of the New Testament One-Anothers on pages 165-166 of this book.

Being Spiritual Together

Who you are as a couple can be infinitely more beautiful and wonderful when you are spiritual together. Every aspect of your relationship will be better. Your spirituality can include Bible reading, singing praise songs and hymns, praying, and going to church. Some couples fast, memorize Bible verses, and talk about the beauty in the world and the universe. There are many ways to pursue and develop spiritually. The important thing is to make a plan, and that you do it together.

When my wife and I were visiting some friends, the husband asked If I wanted to go to the grocery store with him to pick up a few items, so I did. He and his wife were relatively new Christians so in the car, I asked if he and his wife prayed together.

"No. We did that for a while, but we don't anymore."

"Why? What happened?"

"I got tired of her correcting my grammar when I'm talking to the Lord."

He had a point. Praying and being spiritual together is hard enough. Instead of adding to the difficulty, you need to make it a safe experience by being supportive and accepting. The Lord understands your weaknesses and shortcomings, and he's big enough to tolerate bad grammar.

I know some couples who correct each other's theology when they're praying together. Don't do that. There may be other appropriate times to talk about theology, but not while you're praying. God won't send a lightning bolt if you accidentally say something wrong or misquote the scripture in your prayer. What's important is that you're praying together.

There are some cool benefits to being spiritual. You develop a sensitivity for one another. You're more in sync mentally and emotionally. You're stronger psychologically, and better able to handle life's challenges and obstacles. You start knowing each other in a more comprehensive and more intimate way. Plus, you come to a deeper sense of unity with the Lord and with your spouse. After reading chapter three, you're already aware of the power of unity in your marriage. Unity invites the presence of God, and ignites the power of God in your home.

You'll also discover a greater inner security, joy, and fulfillment in your life. Your sex life will be better, and you'll know first-hand what the apostle meant when he wrote in Philippians 4:7, *the peace of God, which surpasses every thought, will guard your hearts and minds in Christ Jesus.* Accompanying these discoveries will be an inner transformation of character, a connection with the God of the universe, and an ability to overcome temptations and personal weaknesses.

In summary, by growing spiritually, you are able to bring your best self to your mate. That is a priceless gift. And that's when marriage truly becomes heaven on earth.

WisdomBuilt Biblical Principles of Marriage

Discussion Starters

 Key Concept: Spirituality is a gift from God. When a couple pursues their faith together, it opens up a whole new level of fulfillment and sensitivity to one another, helping you be at your best as a person and as a couple.

 Discussion Points:

1. What's your favorite hymn or worship song? And your spouse's favorite?
2. What do you like about the church you attend?
3. Do you have a favorite Bible verse, or book of the Bible?
4. What attracted you to your mate?

 **Dig Deeper:**

1. Is it sometimes uncomfortable to pray out loud when you're with other people? How about when you're with your spouse or your kids? Talk with each other about what you're feeling and thinking at those times.
2. If you and your lover were to create a plan for growing spiritually, what would it include? What spiritual activities would you want to do together?

SEX AND SENSUALITY

*Marriage must be respected by all,
and the marriage bed kept undefiled.*

Hebrews 13:4

God created humans to enjoy sex and sensuality immensely and intensely. Yet, these are to be experienced within marriage. When practiced in this context, it's designed to be a mutually awe-inspiring, powerful experience that carries the full blessing of God.

The goal of sex is usually intercourse, but the goal of sensuality may be to express attraction, show that you care, or to make your partner feel loved. Sex and sensuality both help couples bond together and feel close.

Physical Intimacy: A Gift from God

In essence, sex is about intercourse, and sensuality is about bringing pleasure to each other. Sometimes this includes sex, but many times does not. Sex is making sure you get what you want and need. Sensuality is giving, serving, and pleasing your partner. When combined, sex and sensuality provide an opportunity to experience the whole range of sensual pleasure, demonstrate faithfulness, and practice self-control.

One way of approaching sex and sensuality is to consider them as a gift. We like a gift for a variety of reasons. We like the way it makes us feel. Or, it meets a need. Perhaps we enjoy the experience it brings. The same is true for why God gave us the gift of physical intimacy. It feels good, it meets a need, and we enjoy the experience. Let's face it: it's fun & exciting.

If someone doesn't like sex or sensuality, it's usually because there's been some pain in the experience of it. Somewhere along the way the person might have been abused, mistreated, taken advantage of, ridiculed, betrayed, or abandoned. Or it hurts physically.

If this is the case in your marriage, it might be helpful to talk about it together and to seek professional help, because in a normal, healthy marriage the gift of intimacy is a wonderful part of the relationship, and giving yourself to your partner intimately is one of the most valuable gifts you can give.

If you and your partner will honor your marriage and maintain sexual and sensual purity, you will meet each other's needs and capture each other's imagination. The gift you give each other will be beyond comparison. Choosing to honor your mate and your marriage will always have great results. For Christians, it's an imperative.

Fifth Biblical Principle of Marriage: Sex & Sensuality

Hebrews 13:4 says, *Marriage must be respected by all, and the marriage bed kept undefiled, because God will judge immoral people and adulterers.* The principle taken from this verse is that sexuality and sensuality are best when experienced in a faithful, monogamous marriage. This is because the best relationships are built on love, trust, and communication, and marital infidelity is a violation of all three.

Marriage counselors differentiate between sex and sensuality. Sex is described as intercourse, while sensuality refers to enjoyment received through any of the senses: touching, tasting, looking, listening, or smelling. Both sex and sensuality are part of a healthy love life.

There are several biblical reasons for the gift of sex and sensuality. One of the ways we are like the Creator is the possibility of participating in the creation of new life. One of the miracles of intimacy is that children can be the result. God loves, so he creates us. We love each other, and God enables us to bring children into the world. Unfortunately, some couples are not able to have children, but that doesn't imply God loves them less, or that they don't have the complete image of God.

A powerful reason for sex and sensuality is intimacy and closeness. Another way of expressing this is to know and be known, to have someone who we are close to, that we know well, who we trust, and these dynamics are reciprocal. Besides the physical connectedness, there's an emotional and intellectual connection, as well. When two become one in a good marriage, the unity is emotional, intellectual, spiritual, and physical. But maintaining this intimacy requires intentionality.

Another biblical reason for sex and sensuality is pleasure. God made us sensual beings. Proverbs 5:18-19 gives this blessing: *Let your fountain be blessed, and take pleasure in the wife of your youth. A loving doe, a graceful fawn—let her breasts always satisfy you; be lost in her love forever.* This blessing in the proverb refers to sexual gratification.

The intent is that married couples enjoy the pleasures of sex and sensuality so completely that they get lost, become intoxicated, or stray "deliciously dazed in the ecstasies of lovemaking," as Bruce Waltke writes in his commentary on the Proverbs. Rosenau and others use the term "pleasuring" when discussing the intimate ways husband and wife may touch, caress, and otherwise create pleasant physical experience for one another.

When a couple experiences sex and sensuality lovingly, caringly, and tenderly, there is a sense of wonder and awe that, more than anything else, approaches a spiritual experience. It goes beyond the merely physical in its impact. It meets deep emotional and psychological needs. It brings a release from stress. And, there is a certain therapeutic quality to it, because it includes affirmation, touch, affection, trust, physical release of stress, emotional release of stress, vulnerability, communion, and acceptance. No wonder the world has gone crazy for sex and for sensuality. It's a fantastic experience with amazing results to the body, the mind, and the spirit.

Marriage Should Be Honored

Marriage must be respected by all, and the marriage bed kept undefiled, because God will judge immoral people and adulterers (Hebrews 13:4). There are three statements in this verse. First is that marriage is to be honored and respected. The phrase "by all" in the Greek, *en pasin*, may mean that marriage should be honored by all people, or that every aspect of marriage should be honored. It seems to me that Christians ought to recognize both possibilities, and put them into practice.

You honor or dishonor marriage by how you treat and talk about your own marriage and your own spouse. You also honor or dishonor marriage by how you joke about marriage in general. For example, it's common for sitcoms and stand-up comics to dishonor marriage. I've heard Christian men and women horribly dishonor their mate publicly. I've also seen husbands and wives flirt with other men or women. This is dishonoring your lover.

The next part of the verse says the bed must be kept pure. Interestingly, the Greek word for bed is *koité*, which comes into English as coitus, and refers to intercourse or orgasm. The text contains the metaphor "keep the bed pure." This could be translated into English as "keep coitus pure," "keep intercourse pure," or "keep orgasm pure." Sexuality and sensuality are to be undefiled, pure, and done appropriately. This means it is practiced only in marriage. God's intent is for people to engage in sexual activity only with the person they are married to.

However, if you or your spouse have already had an affair or a one-time sexual encounter with someone else, that doesn't mean your marriage is automatically over. There may be time to repent, recommit to your marriage, and make sure you are faithful from now on. The Lord specializes in healing, forgiving, and restoring people who have messed up.

The verse concludes with the comment that God will judge the immoral. If this verse truly represents the intent of the Divine Creator, then sexual purity is not merely an option. It's a must. The writer to the Hebrews tells us quite plainly that God himself will judge those who are sexually immoral. How you behave is important to the Lord. The secret aspects of your life really do matter. As you'll see in chapter eleven, your sexual behavior matters because you belong to the Lord, and because you belong to your mate.

It might be helpful for you and your spouse talk about what you consider to be appropriate and inappropriate sexual behavior, and what you think might be included in the statement about immorality, because being in agreement is essential when it comes to your love life and the intimacy you share.

Generally speaking, there are no limits to how a married couple might want to express their sexual love for each other. Two guidelines you might want to consider and discuss are that you not do anything that hurts physically, nor anything your partner doesn't enjoy. The reason for these is that the purpose of sex and sensuality is mutual pleasuring, so if something's not pleasant, you might want to avoid it. Or, if one of you enjoys it but the other doesn't, then it may not be something you agree on.

Keep in mind, however, that according to Hebrews 13:4, God is the one who will judge those who are immoral. Christians are not called to condemn anybody. Our role is to love people, befriend them, and set an example for them. In John 3:17, Jesus reminds us that *God did not send His Son into the world that He might condemn the world, but that the world might be saved through Him*. So, if Jesus didn't come to condemn, then we need to make sure we're not condemning anyone, either. According to John 16:8, the Holy Spirit will convict the world of sin. The church needs to stay away from the business of condemning, convicting, and shaming people.

Sex is Beautiful and Wonderful

Dr. Douglas Rosenau teaches that "In a loving relationship, enjoying sexuality and connecting with a mate are gifts each brings to the other willingly – not by demands or coercion." You'll recall his ten *Reasonable Biblical Expectations in Christian Marriage*. In the previous chapter, I commented on the expectation of shared spirituality. In this chapter, the focus is on the expectation of "regular, satisfying sexual interaction."

According to Rosenau, "Lovemaking is a cycle of physical and emotional arousal that helps us understand the importance of letting it be an unfolding series of changes." He cites the research of Masters and Johnson, who describe the four-phase cycle of love-making. These four phases are excitement, plateau, orgasm, and resolution.

While it's not my intent to explain the four phases of intimacy in this work, it might be a good idea for pastors and congregational leaders who are called to help married couples, to read Rosenau's book. He does a good job explaining what is happening physically during each phase, and how partners can understand each other and help each other experience the most pleasure. "Every wise lover should understand this basic knowledge in order to focus energy on any neglected phase. Every phase needs a balanced amount of attention."

The fact is, something can go wrong in any of the phases. Couples who are not aware of this fact may never figure it out. Pastors and congregational leaders who aren't aware of this might miss some opportunities to help the couples in their ministry, and may miss some opportunities to save some marriages, because couples who are not finding fulfillment in marriage tend to start looking elsewhere to find it.

Developing or Restoring Sensuality

Unfortunately, physical intimacy tends to diminish over time. Busyness and stress take a toll on every marriage. If you want your marriage to survive and thrive, therefore, you will be intentional about maintaining intimacy. PREP talks about "protecting your sensual relationship" and "protecting your sexual relationship." It's important to talk about and understand the similarities and the differences between the two aspects of physical intimacy so you can make the time for both in your relationship. There are six keys for developing marital sensuousness.

- First is playfulness. When couples meet, date, and fall in love, they are usually quite playful. After being married for a while, however, the seriousness of life beats the playfulness out of them. They become routine with each other, stressed out, often angry, and start looking for other people they can play with.

Making the joint decision to restore playfulness in the relationship can bring back the joy of being together and revive your love life.

- Second is knowledge. I recommend couples do something every year to improve their marriage. Read a book, attend a marriage retreat or seminar, watch a video, participate in a couples class or small group, see a pastor or counselor. This keeps new information and ideas flowing into the relationship, and can prevent staleness from setting in.

- Third is honest communication. Healthy, growing couples talk about everything together, and they do it in a way that builds each other up and affirms each other. They tell each other what they like and don't like when it comes to sex, television, music, food, and humor. They share their secrets, fears, and dreams with each other. We'll discuss this more in chapter nine.

- Fourth is creative romance, both husband and wife taking the time to think creatively about the couple's sex life and sensuality. Plan romantic dates and interesting sexual encounters with each other. Touch each other, even when not in bed.

- Fifth, it is important that the couple try to be physically fit and well-rested. It's tough to enjoy sex and sensuality when you're not at your best.

- Sixth is mutual pleasuring. Dr. John Gottman uses the term "Love Maps" when discussing "the part of your brain where you store important information about your partner's life. These maps hold details about your partner's life history, daily routines, likes, and dislikes." Mutual pleasuring happens when husband and wife know what feels good to each other, when they make the time, and are intentional about creating pleasure for each other. We'll go into this further in chapter eight.

Walking and Talking

My wife and I like to take walks together. It gives us a chance to talk, and for at least a little while, get away from the phone, the noise, and the routines that demand our attention. We got into the habit of taking two or three discussion questions on little slips of paper. While taking an afternoon walk one day, Linda said, "Thank you for never having an affair."

Wow! Where'd that come from?

"You're welcome." I was intrigued as to what had been going through her mind.

After a while she continued. "The other day I heard about another Christian couple getting a divorce because one of them had an affair. It brings so much destruction and devastation, not only to the couple, but to their children, and also their church. I just wanted to thank you for never doing that to me and our sons." During the conversation, we talked about the fact that everyone is tempted.

Growing up in the church, I heard about the typical sins that destroy marriage and ministry. The big three problems are alcohol, sex, and money. I heard similar stories when I was in Bible College and seminary. Therefore, part of my ordination vow was never to have an affair, never steal from someone or from the church, and never get drunk. I made a similar promise to my wife while we were engaged. So far, I've been faithful to those vows.

Sexual Temptation

Even though I'm not the handsomest guy in the world, I've had to deal with sexual temptation. I got a call from a woman in the church who wanted marriage counseling on a Sunday night after church. I thought that was a strange time to want marital counseling, and her husband wasn't planning to come, so I called one of my deacons to ask if he'd be willing to stay after church. I didn't want to be there alone with her.

Sure enough, she didn't want counseling. She wanted me. What she had in mind was for us to take a cruise somewhere, just get away together for about six months, and have lots of sex. I told her I wasn't going to do that. My wife, my sons, and my reputation were more important to me. She persisted, so I told her there was a church board member in the next room. "I'm going to go get him. I suggest that you be gone by the time we get back."

In the Army there were many opportunities to have an affair, because Soldiers spend a lot of time away from home, and we get lonely. One day an attractive Army nurse came into my office and said, "You know we're going to the same conference next week. Why don't we stay in the same hotel room?"

"No, that's not going to happen." I don't do that.

Her next comment is what surprised me. "I'm a Christian too, you know. And it's OK for Christians to have affairs."

"Well, that's not the way I read the Bible, nor is it the way I treat my wife. I don't live that way."

People who travel for their business face similar temptations and opportunities. It helps to have your mind made up before the temptation happens, to have a plan, and maybe an accountability partner. The Bible says Jesus was tempted in every way we are tempted, yet was without sin. It's what you do with the temptation that matters.

Roy Williams has a website for businessmen called The Monday Morning Memo. Each day he discusses a different business topic or theme. On October 6, 2008 he ran a piece called *Husbands Who Cheat*. Here is the article, used with permission.

Husbands Who Cheat

Sex and Sensuality

Listen. No, We're Not Talking About Advertising Today.

I recently had dinner with a young friend who has been married for about a year. When he said that he and his wife were hoping to have a child, I knew it was time for The Talk.

An older friend gave me The Talk twenty-eight years ago when Pennie was pregnant with Rex, our oldest. Since then, I've never failed to pass it along when I hear that a man is about to become a first-time father.

"Everything you hear about the joys of fatherhood are true," I said, "but if you're not ready for the backlash it can knock you off your feet and screw up the rest of your life." He gave me a quizzical look so I continued. "Men who cheat on their wives usually do so for the first time shortly after the birth of their first child."

His quizzical look intensified. "But that doesn't make any sense."

I spoke to him matter-of-factly, like a judge pronouncing judgment on the accused. "You become invisible on the day your baby is born. You remain invisible for nearly a year. You exist only for carrying things. All conversations revolve around the baby. No one asks you about your day. Friends and family walk past you to get to the baby. You're effectively an outcast. You can't complain that the baby gets all the attention. That would make you look like a jerk. Your wife is always tired and distracted. Days turn into weeks. You feel like you've been dumped by your girlfriend. You're lonely. Then a girl smiles at you at work. You haven't seen that in awhile. And she laughs at all your witty remarks. She pays attention to you…"

My friend's mouth opened a little as his jaw slackened. "Wow."

And that, dear reader, is what's known among men as The Talk.

Helping a young man past the crisis of his first child is easy. What's tough is counseling a mature husband who finds himself attracted to another woman.

Dr. Richard D. Grant is a clinical psychologist on the board of directors at Wizard Academy. Here's some advice he gave a roomful of men recently in Tuscan Hall:

"When you find yourself attracted to a woman who is not your wife, sit down with a pen and paper and make a list of the things you like best about the woman. Then look at those attributes as action items on a 'To Do' list for self-improvement. It's never really about the woman. It's about what's missing in your own life."

Dr. Grant then told a story about taking his sons to get a haircut when they were young. "...out of the backroom comes a young woman with scissors in her hand, tan, taut, perky, athletic, windblown, outdoorsy. I was spellbound. So I grabbed a pen and starting writing like mad. Then, looking at the list of her attributes, it hit me: 'I've been working feverishly on a book for months, buried in a manuscript. I'm in need of exercise, sunshine, the outdoors.' So I made a commitment to myself to pursue those things aggressively. Thirty minutes later I left that barbershop with two freshly groomed sons and a To Do list for self-improvement. I never looked back."

Among the 40,000 readers of the Monday Morning Memo there are certain to be many for whom today's memo brought back memories of past heartaches. For this, I apologize.

My goal is not to turn your eyes to the past, but to the future.

Sex and Sensuality

SUMMARY: Guys, we're always attracted to what's missing in our lives. And the thing we miss most will sometimes show up in the form of a woman.

So if you are married but attracted to another woman, grab a pen and paper. Make a list. Get to work on yourself. This is the path that leads to lasting satisfaction.

WisdomBuilt Biblical Principles of Marriage

Discussion Starters

 Key Concept: God wants married couples to enjoy the pleasure of sex and sensuality so completely that they get lost, become intoxicated, or stray "deliciously dazed in the ecstasies of lovemaking."

 Disussion Points:

1. Where did you go on your honeymoon. Besides sex, what did you do?
2. Do you and your spouse talk about your sex life? Why or why not?
3. Has your husband or wife honored you in a way that made you feel good?
4. How do you play together?

 **Dig Deeper:**

1. Do you have a plan for overcoming sexual temptation?
2. Take another look at the *Reasonable Biblical Expectations in Christian Marriage* on page 49. Do you have similar expectations? Are they being fulfilled?
3. Have you made any promises to God or to your mate?

ARE WE HAVING FUN YET?

There is an occasion for everything, and a time for every activity under heaven: a time to weep and a time to laugh; a time to mourn and a time to dance;

Eccl. 3:1, 4

A joyful heart is good medicine, but a broken spirit dries up the bones.

Proverbs 17:22

This scenario happens too often. John and Fran liked each other as soon as they met, so they started dating. They did all kinds of fun activities. They went hang gliding, saw movies, and went to concerts. They discovered they both liked to ski, loved the same music, and enjoyed talking about the Bible. They had fun together. They laughed often. They made life feel good for anyone who was around. It was obvious to them and their friends that they were meant to be together, so they got married. They were best friends.

As they settled into their new life together, the dating gradually stopped. Life got serious, and they forgot the importance of having fun together.

Sixth Biblical Principle of Marriage: Having Fun Together

As a pastor and then as a military chaplain, I've conducted more than two hundred weddings. Almost every time I ask an engaged couple what drew them together and what they like about each other, invariably their answer is that they are best friends. They have fun together, they laugh together, and they want to be together all the time.

People are wired for fun, to enjoy life. We love to laugh, experience new things, and have adventures. We tend to gravitate toward people who are fun to be with, who want to do things we like to do. When a couple keeps on having fun together, their marriage tends to stay fresh, they continue to like each other, and they don't have to look elsewhere for satisfaction. But when a couple stops having fun together, their marriage is headed for trouble.

Why is this the case? Simply because having fun is one of the top three major areas of fulfillment in human experience. People everywhere need spiritual fulfillment. There is a strong, almost universal desire for sexual fulfillment. And everyone needs to have fun in order to enjoy life. When you combine spirituality, sexuality, and fun, you create a life that is deeply satisfying and meaningful. When you do that in your marriage, the result is an amazing marriage and home life. This is the treasure called *Fulfillment*.

What Did You Do Before Getting Married?

Think back to the time just before you got married. Can you remember the things you did together? Who planned the dates? Where did you go? Did you have fun together?

While My wife and I were dating, we would go to a movie, spend an afternoon at a park, or go to the beach. We played miniature golf, hung out with friends, and played tennis. We played cards with her family, spent a lot of time talking, and went to church. One time, we had a midnight picnic with another couple. The event was planned by the ladies, and was a lot of fun.

After marriage, things begin to change. You finish school, look for jobs, have a few kids, get into debt, and life gets serious and heavy. It seems there's no time or energy or interest in having fun anymore. Some couples just don't have enough money.

It's important, however, that you build fun into your lifestyle. You have to balance the seriousness and responsibility with lightheartedness and fun. You have to make time to play, and you need to do it together, not just with other people.

A Joyful Heart is Good Medicine

One of the verses cited at the start of this chapter says *A joyful heart is good medicine, but a broken spirit dries up the bones* (Proverbs 17:22). There have been several studies that demonstrate the positive health effects of joy and laughter. Other research has shown that the absence of joy and laughter can lead to illness or even early death. Where there is joy, people tend to have hope and reason to go on. But where there is no joy, people give up, sometimes literally.

In the same way, joy and laughter have a positive impact on relationships. When a couple builds fun and playfulness into their relationship, their marriage is healthier and lasts longer.

Howard Markman and Scott Stanley cite several surveys and studies about the importance of fun and leisure activities, and how they affect satisfaction and happiness in marriage. One survey reported that having fun together was the single most important factor in "overall marital satisfaction." Another survey showed that the amount of fun a couple had together directly influenced their commitment and their friendship with each other.

Couples who continue to have fun together are happier and healthier, and their marriages tend to last a lifetime. On the other hand, couples who are too busy to play, or who get out of the habit of dating, or who simply ignore the importance of having fun together—those are the couples headed for trouble. You and your partner can put fun back into your life, and it doesn't have to cost a lot of money. It will require that you are intentional, that you plan, and that you agree that its important.

Adding Fun Back Into the Mix

It's possible that your mate might not want to start having fun again. He or she might think it's childish or irrelevant, or there's not enough time or money. There's also a possibility that your partner likes having fun, but not with you. If any of these situations exist in your relationship, you might want to think carefully about how to approach your mate. You need to talk about it together, but you don't want to push your partner away. Here are some suggestions for how to add fun to your marriage.

Make a list of what you like to do for fun, and then a list of what your partner likes to do for fun. You should identify twenty-five things you like to do, and at least ten that your spouse likes to do. Then share your lists with each other and see how many activities you named on each other's list. Were there any surprises?

After sharing the lists, talk about a plan to start doing some of those things together. You might be able to do one of them every week, or on a weekend. Other activities might need more time and expense, and might need to be done during a vacation or extended trip. Take turns planning your activities. It doesn't always have to be the guy who plans a date. Nor should it always be the gal. By taking turns, you share the responsibility, and you share the excitement.

Consider having a weekly date night. You can either plan them together, or take turns deciding what you'll do this week. Depending on your family circumstances, this might involve arranging childcare or rescheduling your work. But your marriage is worth it. In planning your dates, be sure to balance things you've done before, with brand new experiences.

Buy a new game, and invite some friends over to play with you. This can be a lot of fun, but if you get the wrong kind of game, you might add a lot of stress or anxiety. So, work on this together to make sure it's something you'll both enjoy.

A Few Guidelines

Markman and Stanley offer a few guidelines for how to keep it fun. First, try not to get into a rut. When planning for fun together, it's better to include a variety of activities and experiences. Some should be indoors, and some outdoors. Some should be athletic, and some should be cultural. Some should be at night, while others during the day. Some shouldn't cost anything, but some will be expensive. Therefore, it takes careful planning and thinking through what you want to do and what you can afford to do.

Second, make sure you're both having fun, not just one of you. By knowing what each other likes, and by planning together, you can accomplish this.

Third, Protect your fun time from conflict or problem solving. Out on a date, on a picnic, at your friend's house for a bar-b-que, or on a cruise, is not the time to bring up problems. In chapter nine we'll talk about fighting and problem solving. There's an appropriate time and place for it. Just not during your fun time, not during your date night, and not during sex.

Fourth, make time for fun now—not way off in the future. And make sure you do something fun together often.

Linda and I try to do something fun at home every day. We try to have a date or an activity away from home every week. And we try to do something larger once or twice a year. Here's how it works for us.

We start and finish almost every day with a cup of tea and a game of backgammon. We got a game as a wedding gift, learned how to play it, and have a lot of fun with it. We have other games, too, so we'll sometimes pull out one of them. There are several TV shows we like. Plus, we like taking walks together. So, just about every day we'll do at least one of these just for fun. Sometimes, we'll take a walk and watch a TV show. Or maybe watch a movie and then play backgammon.

On the weekend, we like going to a movie, a play, a concert, or to a regional park. Linda keeps a running list of movies that we want to see, so on Friday or Saturday, we'll go out to dinner and then to a show. We also like shopping together, so sometimes we'll include that in our weekend date.

Once or twice a year, depending on work schedules and finances, we like to take a trip or do something more extravagant than the typical date night. On our twenty-third anniversary I took my wife out for dinner, and somewhere during the evening I asked the question: "Where would you like to be two years from right now?"

She responded with a one-word question, "Anywhere?"

"Well, yeah. Where would you like to go for our twenty-fifth?"

Another one-word reply, "England!"

Are We Having Fun Yet?

We planned and saved and thought about it for two years, and when the time came, we had a lot of fun. It was special. We even threw in a weekend in Paris.

Several years ago, we found out one of our favorite singing groups was going to be performing on a cruise to Alaska. We'd never done a cruise, but we looked at each other and our eyes bugged, and we made the decision to do it. It was a special experience in many ways.

Ecclesiastes chapter three says *There is an occasion for everything, and a time for every activity under heaven: a time to weep and a time to laugh; a time to mourn and a time to dance.* A wise couple, who wants to make sure their marriage is happy and filled with satisfaction, will build into the fabric of their relationship a balance of activities that adds the laughter and the dancing to their life together. They'll play, explore, laugh, and learn. They'll help each other pursue and fulfill their dreams. They'll do what it takes to keep growing individually and as a couple. They'll handle the responsibilities of life, but be sure to blend in enough fun. And in so doing, build a life of love, laughter, and meaningful memories.

WisdomBuilt Biblical Principles of Marriage

Discussion Starters

 Key Concept: Having fun together is crucial to building a life of satisfaction and fulfillment.

 Discussion Points:

1. What's one of your favorite memories of your pre-marriage dating and getting acquainted?
2. Identify three things you and your spouse like to do together, other than sex.
3. Do you have any routines, patterns, or traditions for having fun together?
4. When's the last time you laughed together?

 **Dig Deeper:**

1. When you're trying to have fun together, how do you protect the experience from arguing or talking about problems?
2. Is having fun together something you and your partner tend to agree on, or is it another area of disagreement? Would your spouse give the same answer?

TREASURE #3: INSIGHT

Insight empowers you to be more productive in everything you do. Plus, it opens the door to greater intimacy. But more than that, the *Biblical Principles of Marriage* contribute towards healing the heart, soothing the inner hurts, and setting the broken bones of your spirit.

Shalom is a Hebrew term that, on the surface, means "peace." But it's so much more than that, because it refers to the whole person. Shalom, therefore, is a comprehensive condition of the body, the mind, and the spirit.

When you as a couple live these principles every day, you'll experience an inner healing that changes you from the inside out, resulting in new ways of looking at and experiencing the outside world. You will have the shalom of the Lord, the peace that passes understanding.

YOU'VE GOT A FRIEND IN ME

This is my love, and this is my friend.

Song of Songs 5:16

There's nothing as thrilling as having a great lover, and nothing as encouraging as having a good friend. The verse above, from the Song of Songs, says you can have both in your marriage. If you recall, Douglas Rosenau includes friendship as one of the ten reasonable expectations in a Christian marriage: *a best friend offering unconditional love, understanding, and support.*

You've Got A Friend in Me

"You've Got a Friend in Me" was the theme song of the Toy Story animated films from Pixar and Disney. In the story, the song refers to the friendship between Woody and his fans on his original TV show, *Woody's Roundup*. But it's also about Woody (a toy) and Andy (the boy who owns him). And third, it represents the relationship between the two toys, Woody and Buzz. In many ways, the song ties the storyline together. The theme of friendship resonated with millions of moviegoers, because everyone needs meaningful friendship.

In 2013, Michael Bublé recorded the song, but his version, which got up to number ten in the charts, turns it into a love song, and I really like the modified message. It works as a love song.

Seventh Biblical Principle of Marriage: Friendship

This principle is all about building and maintaining a friendship with the person you're married to. In the *Song of Songs*, sometimes called the *Song of Solomon*, the young woman describes her lover to her friends, and in 5:16 says, *This is my love, and this is my friend.*

This is my love, and this is my friend? Yes. In a great marriage, husband and wife are careful to maintain a friendship in addition to their romance, because both are essential.

Don't Be A Jerk

Dr. John Van Epp, in his book *How to Avoid Falling in Love with a JERK*, says falling in love is "a core ingredient in the making of a long-term romance, but it also required the building of a strong friendship." According to Van Epp, the purpose of dating and courting is to build a solid foundation of friendship, trust, and reliance. If done properly, these dynamics of the relationship will continue throughout the marriage. On the other hand, where there is no friendship, trust, or the ability to rely on one another, your marriage is in trouble.

Markman and Stanley indicate the importance of friendship in their PREP materials. Friendship is crucial to a good marriage, but the various roles, responsibilities, obligations, and problems of life can gradually bury the friendship if you're not careful. Life is hard. Making ends meet isn't easy. Balancing marriage, careers, kids, and other commitments adds stress and keeps you too busy. Sometimes it seems there's no time or energy left, so friendship gets buried, pushed aside, taken for granted, or ignored.

Friends are an important part of your life, increasing your chances of being happy, and marriage should add to this quality of life and happiness. However, some couples don't treat each other like friends. Too many husbands and wives violate the very principles of friendship that are designed to show them how to make their marriage successful and happy. Even Dr. Phil stresses the importance of friendship. In his book *Relationship Rescue* he says one of the "foundational values that quickly disappears in a distressed relationship is friendship. To put it simply, you forget to act like friends with your partner."

So, how exactly do friends act together? A recent survey by Reachout.com asked people what they thought a friend was, and how a friend acted and talked. The responses:

A good friend is someone who:
- you can trust won't judge you
- won't deliberately hurt your feelings, but will show kindness and respect
- will love you not because they feel they have to, but because they choose to
- you can depend on, who is loyal and whose company you enjoy
- will be there no matter what your situation is
- is trustworthy and not afraid to tell you the truth, no matter how hard it is sometimes
- can laugh when you laugh
- will cry when you cry
- makes you smile
- accepts you for who you are, and lends an ear when you need to whine or complain
- will give you room to change

Let's take a closer look at these characteristics of friends.

A Friend is Someone Who Won't Judge or Criticize

I was visiting a couple in their home, and throughout the evening, the guy was criticizing his wife, telling her she never did anything right, and doing his best to humiliate her. It was a really bad scene, pretty uncomfortable. That's unacceptable. That's not what love is about. I sat in another home where both husband and wife complimented each other often, and made only positive, encouraging comments the entire time. It was genuine, created a warm atmosphere, and put me at ease. I enjoyed spending time with them.

A Friend is Someone Who Doesn't Try to Hurt You

I was teaching a class at a Christian university when a young lady in the front row asked a question that was totally unrelated to the lesson. She asked me in front of twenty-two other students, "Have you ever hurt your wife?"

"Yes, I have."

The student was devastated, and gasped audibly. "No!"

I thought I'd better tell her the story rather than leave her disillusioned. "When we were newlyweds, we lived in an apartment complex. One night, we were down at the pool, and as we were drying off, my young wife snapped me with her towel.

Now, in the family I grew up in, that's a challenge and an invitation to a friendly battle. So, I got my towel and snapped her back. My bride grabbed the towel and wrapped it around her finger, but I didn't see that. When I yanked the towel back, I broke her finger. So technically, I have hurt my wife. But I never hurt her on purpose."

My student gave a deep sigh of relief. She wanted to believe I was a Christian man who treated his wife properly, and she was glad to hear I hadn't hurt my wife on purpose.

Someone Who Loves You and is Kind to You By Choice

In the business world, politics, and the social scene, a lot of people pretend to be nice. They play the game because that's what's expected, or they're attempting to get ahead, make the sale, or get the job. A friend, on the other hand is nice to you all the time, even when there's nothing to gain. Ephesians 4:32 says, *Be kind and compassionate to one another, forgiving one another, just as God also forgave you in Christ*. Christians make the effort to be genuine in their kindness. The same is true of the way good husbands and wives treat each other.

A Friend is Someone You Can Depend On

Do you and your spouse keep your word to each other? When you say you'll do something, do you follow through? And do you go above and beyond the expectation? That's what love does.

When our youngest son was in the sixth grade, he wanted to participate in the annual sixth-grade trip. My wife asked if I would stop by the school and sign him up, reminding me that this was the last day to sign up our son so he could get in on the experience. No problem; I'll do it. But on the way to work, I started listening to some music, and forgot to stop by the school. Mid-morning, I realized my mistake, and decided I would take care of it on my way home from work. No problem . . . I thought.

At around 11:00 a.m. Linda called me at the office. "I just want to make sure you took care of signing him up."

"Yes, I did." I figured I would be sure to do it on the way home from work, and she'd never know I forgot.

But, wanting to make sure her son was taken care of, my dear wife called the school to see if he was on the roster, and the woman in the office told her, "I'm sorry, Mrs. Linzey, but your husband didn't stop by to sign him up." When Linda called me back, it was clear that I had lied to her. I left work immediately to take care of what I had agreed to do.

It would have been better had I not lied in the first place. That was a hard lesson to learn. I was humiliated. But Linda was gracious and forgiving. Fortunately, that's the only time I ever lied to her. I want her to know she can depend on me. But if lying had become a lifelong pattern, you can imagine the damage it would do to our marriage.

A Friend is Someone You Choose to Be With Because You Like Each Other

A good friend of mine is struggling in her marriage because her husband would rather be out with his friends than with her. Notice I said, "out with his friends." She's not one of them. That's a sure signal that the marriage is headed for trouble. A different friend and her husband love spending time together. They have plenty of friends that they do things with, but their preference is to be together.

A Friend is Loyal Regardless of the Situation

As we discussed in principle number two, when you're married, your loyalty has to shift to your mate. Your partner must believe that your loyalty is to the marriage first, more than to other family, other friends, career, or hobbies. Do that, and you prove your love real fast.

A Friend is Someone You Can Trust

Do you feel safe with each other? Do you feel safe confiding in each other? That's the goal in a good relationship. You shouldn't have to give each other the Miranda Warning that police officers read or cite when they have a suspect. *You have the right to remain silent. Anything you say will be used against you.*

Some couples live with the fear that their words will be used against them, so they're always walking on egg shells. Friends, that's no way to live as a couple.

A Friend Laughs With You When You're Happy, and Cries With You When You're Sad

Empathy is a key to a good friendship. To feel what each other feels and provide support demonstrates that you care, that you're interested, and that you are a safe confidant. When you're in a conversation together, listening and supporting are more important than problem solving. Too many spouses automatically shift into trying to provide answers, solutions, and fixing things, when what your partner wants and needs is for you just to be there, listen, and encourage.

According to my wife, you need to make all the right sounds: *uh huh, wow, really, oh no, mmm hmmm, oh my goodness.* And then ask the right questions: *How did that make you feel? What happened next? Do you really think so? What do you think you should do about it? Is there any way I can help?*

But above all, avoid trying to be the fixer. Unless your partner asks you to provide input, suggestions, or recommendations . . . don't do it. Your job as a friend is to be there, listen, and understand, not be the answer-person. Nobody likes a friend who is a know-it-all or who always has to provide the answers and solutions.

A Friend Accepts You Just the Way You Are

A true friend accepts you without trying to change you. After all, you liked each other enough to fall in love and get married. So, don't try to force each other into a mold after the wedding. There are nice ways to express preferences and suggestions, but you need to accept each other, and trust the Lord to help you grow, mature, and become the people you are meant to be. Life has a way of shaping and changing you. Your role as a friend is to be a support as it's happening, because it might be a painful process. Trying to change your spouse might make it worse. Therefore, unless your lover asks you your opinion, it's better not to offer it.

A Friend is There to Listen When You Need to Talk

Have you ever asked a friend if you could get together because there were some things you needed to talk about? But when you got together, your friend did all the talking, and you never got to say what was on your mind? Husbands and wives do that to each other sometimes. Please keep in mind that it's more important in your marriage to listen than it is to speak.

Sure, there's a balance that each couple has to negotiate, but when your mate wants to talk, express an emotion, or think out loud, your role is just to be a listener and a sounding board.

A Friend is a Sounding Board

A couple years ago, my wife and I went to a museum that had a display of antique musical instruments. The docent gave the history of many of the instruments, and talked about the importance of a sound board, especially for stringed instruments. The principle is that the strings vibrate, making the musical notes, but by themselves, might not be loud enough for the audience to hear. However, when the strings are placed on or near a sheet of wood or a solid box, the vibrations transfer, and the sound is amplified.

The guide demonstrated this with a small, wind-up, music box mechanism that wasn't in a box. When she turned the handle, the music played faintly, barely perceptible. Then she placed it up against a wooden cabinet. This time the music was loud, and easily heard throughout the room.

That's what a good friend is like. To listen to your thoughts, your fears, your hopes, your stories, and your music. Not to change you, correct you, or criticize you, but to hear you and help you hear yourself.

Putting these aspects of friendship together, you get a feel for the role a good friend can have in your life. A good friendship is egalitarian, offers enjoyable companionship and shared activities. It includes affection and a chance for stress-free conversation. No wonder there's evidence that people with good friends are happier, healthier, and live longer. That's what a good marriage does for you, too.

There are two verses in Proverbs 18 that are usually considered separately, but I want you to look at them together. The first is, *A man who finds a wife finds a good thing and obtains favor from the Lord* (Proverb 18:22). The second is, *A man with many friends may be harmed, but there is a friend who stays closer than a brother* (Proverbs 18:24).

Verse twenty-two is reminiscent of Genesis 2:18, where God looks at the man he made and says it's not good for him to be alone. If you remember the verse in Genesis, God uses the term *helper* for the mate. Having a wife or a husband as a helper is a good thing.

Preachers often read verse twenty-four, and immediately start talking about Jesus, who is a friend who is often closer than any earthly friend or family member. It is definitely true that Jesus is your friend. We see this in John 15:13-15, where Jesus calls his disciples his friends.

However, there's another way of looking at the Proverb. The word "friends" in the first part of verse 24 can be translated as *friends, companions, neighbors,* or *acquaintances.* But in the second part of the verse, the word used for the *friend who sticks closer than a brother* is sometimes translated as *lover, true friend,* or *most loyal friend.* In this light, it's quite possible to see verse 24 as a contrast between a person who has many acquaintances, as opposed to someone who has one true friend, a loyal lover . . . the wife of verse 22.

In her book, *A Marriage Without Regrets,* Kay Arthur tells of a woman's magazine that asked married men *what was the glue that held their marriage together.* Of the men who answered, 59% said the glue that held their marriage together was friendship.

John Gottman's research points to the fact that when a couple likes each other, when their friendship is intact, there's a dynamic that he refers to as "positive sentiment override." This is a tendency to believe the best in each other. When something is said that might be taken as positive or negative, a couple with a highly developed, quality friendship will interpret it as positive. Because of the love, the trust, and the history of being supportive, they're able to take in stride the give and take of daily life without getting bent out of shape or focusing on the negative. Gottman goes on to offer "the simple truth that happy marriages are based on a deep friendship."

He goes on to say that for 70% of the wives included in his research, the determining factor whether they feel satisfied in their marriage is the quality of the couple's friendship. And for men, it's exactly the same: 70%. In this regard, men and women are remarkably alike.

Love Accentuates the Positive

First Corinthians 13:4-8 says, *Love is patient, love is kind. Love does not envy, is not boastful, is not conceited, does not act improperly, is not selfish, is not provoked, and does not keep a record of wrongs. Love finds no joy in unrighteousness but rejoices in the truth. It bears all things, believes all things, hopes all things, endures all things. Love never ends.*

In essence, that kind of love becomes possible when friendship is established in the relationship. That's how Jesus loves you. And he empowers you, so you can love others the same way . . . especially your marriage partner.

Discussion Starters

 Key Concept: In a great marriage, husband and wife are best friends who offer unconditional love, acceptance, understanding, and support.

 Discussion Points:

1. Do you and your spouse have a favorite song or a favorite singer?
2. Which developed first for you: romance or friendship?
3. When was the last time you felt "buried" by responsibilities, obligations, and busy-ness?

 Dig Deeper:

1. *Do not share this answer in a group setting. If you're in a group discussion, you may simply say yes or no. But you should talk about this with your partner.*
   Are there any aspects of friendship discussed in this chapter that you feel might be lacking in your marriage?
2. Does *positive sentiment over-ride* describe the way you and your spouse interpret routine comments and experiences? If not, what can you do about that?

YADA, YADA, YADA

Adam was intimate with his wife Eve, and she conceived and gave birth.

Genesis 4:1

The April 24, 1997 episode of the Seinfeld Show was titled *the Yada, Yada*. Neither Jerry Seinfeld nor the show's writers coined the phrase "yada, yada;" it was already in use. But after being included on the show, the expression skyrocketed in popularity, and is still used by a lot of people.

There's some debate about the origin of the phrase. Some say it's from the English expression *yatter*, while others say it comes from the Norwegian *jada*, which is pronounced the same and means the same as yada. Other sources say it comes from Yiddish or Hebrew. In any case, it usually means the same as *blah, blah, blah*, or *et cetera, et cetera, et cetera*. Instead of reciting the boring details of a story, you say *yada, yada, yada* instead.

When you watch the *Yada, Yada* episode, however, it's quite obvious from the way the characters tell their stories that there's a sexual connotation and an intentional double meaning going on. Apparently, there is some evidence that *yada* is, indeed, a euphemism for sex. If so, when the Seinfeld cast says *yada, yada, yada* in those stories, what they're really saying is *sex, sex, sex*. Watch it on YouTube and see if it seems that way to you.

Because people are sometimes shy about discussing sex, we often use euphemisms when talking about it. Some of those expressions are *making love, going all the way, doing it, hanky-panky,* and *hitting a home run.* My sister and her husband use the phrase *twice around the park* when referring sex. My wife and I use a different term.

Our teen-aged son never wanted to talk when we wanted to; he always waited 'til late at night. When we were way past ready to go to bed . . . that's when he was just coming alive and wanted to talk. One night he asked, "Hey guys. Wha'd you do on your honeymoon?" I have no idea what brought that question to his mind, or what he expected us to say.

There's a lot of things we did on our honeymoon, but the one that came to mind was, "Well, Son. We played backgammon. Someone gave us a backgammon game as a wedding gift, and we took it with us. We stopped at a store and bought some instructions, and learned to play the game while on our honeymoon."

"Oh. Okay." Apparently, that satisfied his curiosity for the time being.

Two weeks later, we were in our bedroom with the door closed, but still fully clothed, playing backgammon on the bed, when there was a knock on the bedroom door. Same son wanted to talk.

"Dad, can we talk about something?"

"Sure, Son. Come on in."

When he opened the door and saw us on the bed, his jaw dropped, eyes opened wide. "Oh my gosh! You really do play backgammon!"

"What did you think I meant?"

"Uh . . . I thought you made it up cause you didn't want to talk about what you really did on your honeymoon!"

"Oh! Well, we really did play backgammon."

"Oh. My. Gosh."

Ever since that conversation, *backgammon* has been a euphemism for sex in our family. "So that's what you did on your honeymoon, heh heh."

Yada = Knowing

When Genesis 4:1 says *Adam was intimate with his wife Eve*, the word translated as *intimate* is the Hebrew word *yada*. The Hebrew Bible, called the *Tanach*, from the Jewish Publication Society translates this verse, *Now the man knew his wife Eve, and she conceived and bore Cain*. The word *knew* has a footnote that says, *Heb. yada, often in a sexual sense*. Following the Jewish understanding of *yada* in this context, many English translations of Genesis 4:1 keep the idea to *know*. The word means to "know intimately, to know completely, to be familiar." No wonder one of its additional meanings is *to know sexually*.

Other translations render the verse as follows. These are all appropriate ways to translate Genesis 4:1, where it says in Hebrew, *Adam yada'd his wife*.

- Adam and Eve had a son.
- The man knew his wife.
- Adam had sexual intercourse with his wife.
- Adam slept with his wife.
- Adam had relations with his wife.
- Adam made love to his wife.

One of John Gottman's *Seven Principles for Making Marriage Work* is what he calls *Love Maps*. Couples with a strong, resilient marriage not only know each other, they know a lot about each other. "From knowledge springs not only love but the fortitude to weather marital storms. Couples who have detailed love maps of each other's world are far better equipped to cope with stressful events and conflict."

I met Dr. Gottman when he spoke at Rollins College in Orlando a few years ago. During a private conversation about love maps, he said it's not an accident that the word *know* is used for sexual intimacy in Genesis 4:1. Knowing each other is crucial to maintaining a satisfying love life.

Eighth Biblical Principle of Marriage: Knowing Each Other

Linda and I met in college and liked each other right away, but we didn't know how to start or grow a healthy relationship. Fortunately, one of her professors gave his students a list of one hundred questions with this statement, "If you want a relationship to work out, these are the questions you need to ask each other."

I was nineteen, and had been praying about finding a girlfriend. Linda was seventeen, and interested in dating a Christian guy. We met in the campus cafeteria. That night was a freshman class pizza party, and we "managed" to sit next to each other. I really wanted this new relationship to last a lifetime. OK, I'll admit it. I knew early in the relationship that I wanted to marry her. She wasn't sure at first!

When she showed me the list of questions her teacher gave the class, we decided to go to the park near her home to talk about the issues included in the questionnaire. It took us a few weeks to cover all one hundred questions, but, wow, did we learn a lot about each other. And we fell in love.

Years later, when I was in graduate school, I had to complete two personality inventories. Each one contained hundreds of questions, and before turning them in to the instructor, I copied the questions, and we started taking one or two questions with us whenever we took a walk together. That way, we had something to talk about, we kept on learning about each other, we understood what was happening on the inside, how we felt about things, plus, how we had grown or changed over the years.

It was fabulous, and had a wonderful impact on our marriage. Knowing each other's past, each other's present, each other's hopes, dreams, and fears has a way of bonding us together.

What's on Your Bucket List

One of the most powerful experiences we've ever had as a couple was when the movie *The Bucket List* came out. We decided that we'd each write a list. Then, we'd go out to dinner on Saturday night to share and talk about the items we included. Doing so was a dynamic experience. It was spiritual. It was profound. We told each other things we'd never talked about, and found out what each other wanted to accomplish in the future. In many ways, it changed and shaped our future. But in a beautifully positive way.

How well do you know your partner? Do you keep secrets? Are there areas of your personal story that are off limits? Do you know each other's friends, where you like to shop, each other's clothing sizes? What about where you work, who you work with, and what you like and don't like about your jobs? Have you talked about what you like and don't like when making love? Or the part about parenting that is hardest or least fun? Are there times when one of you says, "I don't want to talk about it?" Do you say or hear that too often?

Linda's college professor was right. If you want your relationship to last long term and be happy, you need to know a lot about each other. Therefore, you need to start talking. Sharing.

Opening up. This will require a great amount of trust in each other, because if you don't feel safe together, you're not likely to do this. On the other hand, talking together and letting your spouse see you intimately, get to know you personally, and understand you deeply will transform your marriage.

One of my favorite movies is *Groundhog Day*. Bill Murray plays a self-centered TV weatherman who doesn't care about anyone but himself. Nobody likes him, and he likes nobody. But on assignment in Punxsutawney, Pennsylvania, to cover Groundhog Day, he gets trapped in a cycle of living the same day over and over.

At first, he's angry. But gradually, he begins to see himself as he really is. While he's getting to know himself, he's also starting to know and understand others in the town, what their hopes and dreams are, what makes them tick. In the process, he changes into a generous, helpful, loving person. Once that happens, he breaks free from the time loop, and he is a changed man.

Commitment to Know and Be Known

Your commitment to one another as husband and wife has to be more than just a commitment to stay together. You have to include a commitment to know each other, and allow yourself to be known. To facilitate this, you might need to find some lists of topics or questions to use as a guide.

Marriage encounter has some great questions that help couples get in touch with each other. Their questions have the dual focus of sharing information, and talking about how you feel about that information. You can search online and find hundreds of questions. Do what Linda and I do, and discuss two or three questions at a time. Do that once a week, and after a year, you will have covered a lot of stuff together.

Yada, Yada, Yada

At the end of his chapter on love maps, John Gottman has a helpful section on getting to know each other. He includes a Love Maps Questionnaire, a Love Map 20 Question Game, a guide for making your own love maps, plus several other exercises. In another book, *The Relationship Cure*, Dr. Gottman offers a guide for developing love maps for your children. Friends, with so much good material available, you simply must do what it takes to build a strong marriage, stay together, and stay happy.

But where do you start? Here are seven sample starter ideas for you to consider. My wife and I have done all of these. Not at the same time, of course. But every year we like to do something new, creative, and fun to continue learning about each other, experiencing new places, and trying new activities.

This is because people continue changing throughout their lives. You're not the same person you were five years ago, and neither is your spouse. There's always more to learn about each other. Attitudes change, beliefs change, and habits change. Your body's not the same, you get new friends and lose old ones, and you grow with each additional experience. Hopefully, you're growing wiser and smarter, too.

Some of these activities might cost more than you can afford. If that's the case, then try those that don't cost anything, or not much.

1. Attend a marriage seminar or couples retreat.

These may be offered by a church, a counseling clinic, or a marriage ministry. Some are better than others, of course. Some are more fun. So, you might need to do a little research and ask around before deciding. If you're not sure, you are welcome to email me through my website and ask for a recommendation, or you may ask your pastor or denomination's HQ.

2. Read another book together about developing a great marriage.

Hopefully, you're reading this book together. You might consider looking through the bibliography at the back of this book for the next one to read together. There are some great books listed, but there are so many that I couldn't begin to name them all. Then take time each week to talk about a section of it together.

3. Set aside thirty minutes per week when both of you may ask one or two questions.

This might feel awkward at first, but after doing it a few times, I think you'll enjoy it. It might be a good idea to start with relatively mild questions, and gradually work your way towards the tough issues. You don't want to make it painful on your first try, so don't use this Q&A to bring up wounds, hurts, betrayals, or problems. Instead, make it fun and light, especially at the start. If you do it right, you'll build up enough strength and trust to the point where you can handle the tougher issues.

4. Take a class together . . . any class where you'll learn new info or skills.

In every city there are evening and weekend classes you can take. Sometimes they're at a college or night school. They might be at a church or synagogue. Some businesses offer classes to the public, as do some service clubs. There are classes for learning new skills, hobbies, and recreation. Some people take art classes. A friend of mine used to teach baking classes on Thursday nights at an arts and crafts store. He makes some really good desserts and pastries! And if you can't find a class in your area that you agree on, consider taking an online class. The possibilities are almost endless.

5. Do an online search for "Questions for Couples," and select a questionnaire.

After you agree on a set of questions, take the next few weeks or months to talk about them. Make sure you give time for both of you to answer the questions. In most marriages, one spouse or the other is quicker to talk, answer, and reveal. In our marriage, my wife answers more readily, and I'm quite a bit slower. For some couples, it's the husband who answers fast, and the wife takes more time. Either way is OK. You might consider using the questions at the end of each chapter in this book. Added together, there are 75 discussion starters, and those might be a natural place to begin, since you already have the book.

6. Take a trip to each other's home town.

Seeing where each other grew up can add a lot to your knowledge of each other. If you can, visit your childhood home, the schools you attended, and your old church. Where you played little league or went ice skating. Is the theater still there? Where you got your first job? Do any family friends or relatives still live there? Doing this can potentially bring up some old pain, or some feelings that are uncomfortable, so be ready to support each other. But it can also be therapeutic, or provide some insight that you forgot a long time ago.

7. Once a month, see a movie, a concert, or a play together.

Then go out for dessert or coffee and talk for a couple hours about the topics that were raised in the film, the music at the concert, or the special effects that you observed. When you do this, make sure you don't criticize or make fun of each other for the ideas you share. The goal is to be safe, and when you're safe with each other, you're much more likely to open up, become vulnerable, and let your partner see your real thoughts. The opposite of feeling safe, is being afraid . . . Afraid of what your spouse might think or say or do. That's not the kind of marriage you want. Nor do you want your kids to be afraid. Make your home a safe place. Make your love a safe place. Real love erases fear and soothes the heart, ushering in a freedom to relax, let down your guard, and enjoy life and love.

In his book *Relationship Rescue*, Dr. Phil suggests creating a "Personal Profile" and a "Partner Profile" because by knowing yourself and knowing your partner, you can interact as a couple with more insight and wisdom, and you're better equipped in the relationship.

There's an unlimited number of things you can do to improve your love maps and get to know each other better. By doing some of these activities, you can stay fresh in your relationship instead of getting into a rut. You can keep growing and learning. And in so doing, stay on track to have a better marriage than you ever thought imaginable. The result will put you well on your way to decorating your home with the treasure called *Insight*.

Yada, Yada, Yada

Discussion Starters

 Key Concept: Couples with a strong, resilient marriage know a lot about each other. Insight enables them to weather every storm, and conquer every problem.

 Discussion Points:

1. A euphemism is an expression you use instead of saying something naughty or unacceptable. Do you and your partner have any euphemisms for sex?
2. What were two or three of the first things you knew about your mate?
3. Is there anything you didn't know about your spouse until recently?
4. Do you have a favorite book of the Bible? How about a favorite verse?

 Dig Deeper:

1. What have you and your lover done to get to know each other? What do you think you should do next?
2. On a scale of 1-10, how complete are your marital love maps?
3. *Do not share this answer in a group setting:*
   Is your marriage a safe place? Or do you have some fear that if you were totally open, you might be hurt in some way? If there's some fear, you might want to consider contacting your pastor or counselor.

NOW YOU'RE TALKIN'

Life and death are in the power of the tongue.

Proverbs 18:21

When I came across Deborah Tannen's book, *You Just Don't Understand*, it looked good, so I bought it, took it home, and placed it on my nightstand. That night I picked it up and started reading, and reading, and reading. The more I read, the more I laughed out loud. The subtitle—what it's really all about—is *Men and Women in Conversation*.

"What are you laughing about?" my wife wondered.

"I'm laughing cause she's talking about you and me."

"What?"

How Did She Know?

Every night I read a few more pages, still laughing. I'm sure Dr. Tannen didn't mean for her book to be taken as a comedy. She wrote it as a straight-forward description of the way men and women communicate, based on the way they think and their goals and purposes in the relationship. But when you see yourself and your spouse on every page, it makes you wonder, *How did she know that's what we do?*

I think I learned more about communication with my wife from Tannen's writing than from any other source. It was easy to see my wife's foibles and laugh about them. *Aha! See? That's what you do!* But then to read about what I do was a real eye-opener. I had to own up to my own patterns and behaviors.

What I learned was that Linda and I are pretty normal in how we communicate, and how we fail to communicate. In many ways, we fall into the stereotypes of male and female. But the way Dr. Tannen tells the stories is so funny. I called it my evening devotions. I had to read more.

I wouldn't be offended if you put this book down right now, drive over to your nearest bookstore, and buy Deborah Tannen's book. Or, if you walk over to your computer and order it online. It's that good.

One of the principles she discusses is the asymmetry between the way men and women think and communicate. Men talk to *Report*; women talk to *Rapport*. When there's a problem, men move immediately into Fix-it mode; women move into Affirmation mode. Men speak to establish Hierarchy; women speak to establish Community. Of course, these are generalities. There are men and women at both ends of each spectrum.

Report vs Rapport. Fix-it vs Affirmation. Hierarchy vs Community

Women don't need a fixer. And, contrary to popular myth, they don't want a knight in shining armor to come and rescue them. They want someone they can relate to, someone who will affirm them, someone who takes time to understand.

Men are more comfortable talking about information than relationship. Their standard response to a problem is to come up with a solution, and they don't understand why they're not appreciated for it. They want someone who doesn't read into their words and reinterpret them, but instead will take them at face value.

Now You're Talkin'

A couple years ago, a blogger posted an entry called *Her Diary, His Diary*. Hers was almost 300 words long. His had only seven words. She wrote that her husband was acting weird. He was upset about something, but wouldn't talk about it. She tried to ask if she'd done something wrong, but he just said not to worry about it; it wasn't about her. She was a total wreck by the end of the night, trying to figure it out, and finally concluded their marriage was over and her life was a disaster. His diary that day simply said, *Motorcycle won't start . . . can't figure out why*.

The comments from readers after the post, are just as telling as the original blog. Men sided with the husband. They got it. Women sided with the wife. They understood. Apparently, the writer struck a nerve.

In 1999, newspaper columnist and humorist Dave Berry wrote a classic piece about a man and woman on a date, Roger and Elaine, having a conversation in the car. The guy is concerned about the car, and the gal is worried about the relationship. Their conversation is hilarious, a great example of two people trying to have a discussion, making assumptions, but neither person knowing what the other is even thinking about or talking about.

Linda and I have had conversations like that. It's not funny while it's happening, but later on, it's hilarious to look back, once we finally break through, communicate and understand each other.

Ninth Biblical Principle of Marriage: Words Are Powerful

The ninth *Biblical Principle of Marriage* comes from Proverbs 18:21 and has to do with the way you communicate. *Life and death are in the power of the tongue*. It's important that you talk together regularly. That's how you grow a good relationship. How you talk to each other will make or break your marriage, because words are powerful.

Too often, husbands and wives are careless with their words, giving no thought to what they're doing to their mate. Or worse, some are intentionally cruel with their words, actually trying to hurt, damage, or destroy the one they're supposed to love.

Words can inspire or deflate the person you're talking with. Imagine the impact of hearing your husband or wife telling you every day, *You are wonderful. You're good-looking. You're smart. You can do anything you put your mind to.* Now, imagine what happens if instead, what you hear every day is, *You're dumb. You'll never amount to much. You can't do anything right.*

When our kids were young, we started telling them, *You are talented and creative.* I don't know how many zillion times they heard it, but we told them pretty often, and I think they believed it then, and I think they still do. There's a certain sense of people becoming what they believe. Therefore, it's important that we give the right messages.

Words Have the Power of Life and Death

Words can kill or heal. This is the message of the proverb. Every time you insult, name-call, or say something derogatory to your partner, you are bringing illness or death. It's like your words are a thermostat or volume control. By speaking positives, encouragement, and inspiration, you're turning up hope, confidence, health, and life. But by speaking negatives, discouragement, and insults, you're turning up despair, stress, sickness, and death.

The ramifications are far-reaching, impacting your partner's health, self-confidence, and other relationships. It can affect performance in any area of life: work or school, athletics, driving, or sex. If you're on the same team, you want your teammate to be as healthy as possible. So, you don't want to turn up sickness and death. Instead, you are careful to turn up life, health, and joy. And you do that with your words.

Nonverbal Communication

When I first heard about non-verbal communication, I wondered *What the heck is that all about?* I was at a distinct disadvantage. Women are better at communicating with body language, facial expression, and touch. It was strange territory for me. It wasn't natural at first.

Non-verbal communication means you pay attention and communicate with your body, in addition to your words. You show your lover through touch and action that you're participating in the conversation and the relationship. You look at each other when talking. Your body movements aren't restless. Your touch is gentle and comfortable, not intense or harsh.

One important non-verbal is simply being with each other in silence sometimes. You might be thinking you have to say something, but silence in each other's presence can add a depth of communication that is heart-to-heart, instead of mouth-to-ear.

We've all used non-verbal communication many times. A touch, a smile, a nod, a wink. Thumbs up, A-OK, a "T" for "time out." Stepping out of the way to let someone pass by. Lending a hand without being asked.

Have you ever watched the TV Show "Home Improvement"? One episode was all about "The Look" that a wife can give to her husband. But men are just as effective as women when it comes to giving *the Look*. Maybe you have several "looks."

These non-verbals can communicate huge messages that may be positive or negative. They usually communicate a lot more than words ever could. You've heard the expression, "A picture is worth a thousand words." Or this one, "Don't say you love me... show me!" Non-verbal communication is effective because it communicates on a deeper, emotional level, often leaving an image on the brain and on the heart.

Communicating at the Feeling Level

Feelings are neither right nor wrong, good nor bad. When something happens, or someone does something or says something, emotions happen. It's not productive to try to control or change how you feel. What you can do, however, is control how you express your feelings, because what you do or say may be right or wrong. What you do or say might be good or bad, helpful or harmful, constructive or destructive.

Everyone gets angry once in a while. That's normal. In fact, that's good. It means you're still alive and you still care. But, what do you do when you're angry? Do you attack? Do you say unkind words? Do you throw or break things? Do you strike out and hit the one you say you love? Or, do you use self-control and respond in positive ways, choosing your words and actions carefully?

Have you ever argued before going to church? One Sunday morning we were arguing at home before getting into the car, and we were arguing in the car on the way to the church. When we got to church, we opened the doors, got out of the car, and separated for the morning at church. Afterwards, we met at the car, got in, closed the doors, and picked up the fight right where we left off.

Because feelings are neither right nor wrong, it doesn't help to say, "I shouldn't feel this way," or "You shouldn't feel that way." It's better to try to understand the feelings that are there, and the reasons for them, while controlling your responses to the feelings. When you understand each other's feelings, you have a better chance to relate to each other in ways that bring out the best in each other. In a good marriage, that's the goal—to bring out the best in each other.

Feelings are an important part of a relationship. They give life and energy to a couple's interaction. When done appropriately, sharing feelings with each other builds relationship, but when done inappropriately, the relationship may be in trouble.

Part of Dr. John Gottman's methodology is to ask couples to argue, to fight about real, ongoing conflict in their marriage. He videos their interaction and monitors their physiological reactions. After several years of doing this with couples, he saw a pattern. Arguing doesn't lead to divorce. Anger doesn't lead to a marital meltdown. The clues to marital failure and success "are in the way they argue." In other words, what you do when you are angry is the key, not the fact that you are angry. "Statistics tell the story: 96 percent of the time you can predict the outcome of a conversation based on the first three minutes of the fifteen-minute interaction! A harsh start-up dooms you to failure."

The First Three Minutes of an Argument

But the harsh start-up is only one of the problems Gottman describes. Couples who are angry with each other will move on to other negative interactions: criticism, contempt, defensiveness, stonewalling, screaming, intentionally hurting each other. After engaging in these destructive behaviors, sometimes one spouse will try a *Repair Attempt*. This might be an attempt to back off, ease the tension, make a joke, apologize, or in some way move to end the conflict and return to a positive state.

How the other responds to the *Repair Attempt* is another determinant. According to Gottman, some people have a "crabby habit of mind" or are chronically angry. Whether this is caused physiologically or by one's emotional heritage of the family of origin, this angry frame of mind is often what prevents the *Repair Attempt* to be successful.

Anger a Doorway to Deeper Intimacy

Gary Smalley considers conflict to be a tremendous doorway to intimacy. "But the good news is that we can not only reduce our conflicts, we can also use them to move into deeper intimacy in any relationship. . . . When conflict is used this way, we don't need to be afraid of it; it actually becomes a good thing that moves the relationship forward."

This is why the scriptures don't tell us anger is bad or wrong. Instead, the message from the Word of God is that anger is normal, it's good. It can motivate, inspire, and lead us to action, to problem solving, to accomplishing something for the good.

Ephesians 4:26-27 says, *Be angry and do not sin. Don't let the sun go down on your anger, and don't give the Devil an opportunity.* According to the apostle Paul, there's nothing wrong with anger or any other strong passionate feelings. It's the misuse or misdirection of these emotions that is wrong. Nothing wrong in being angry; but a lot of wrong in expressing that anger destructively.

Gentle Answer vs Harsh Words

Proverbs 15:1 says *A gentle answer turns away anger, but a harsh word stirs up wrath*. This calls for a degree of self-control so you don't bring out the worst in each other, and you don't destroy all the good that's already in your marriage.

Anger isn't bad. Anger isn't sin. Anger isn't of the devil. God designed and created your capacity to become angry in order to empower and motivate you for solving problems, for clearing up misunderstandings, for correcting injustices, and for making sure your family is safe and provided for. You're supposed to use your anger to make things better . . . not worse.

Anger is classified as a power emotion because it's a strong motivator. Anger releases adrenaline and other chemicals that increase your physical strength and mental clarity. Even so, your thoughts and actions must be guided by your values, by the Word of God, and by the Holy Spirit. That's why the Fruit of the Spirit called Self-Control is extremely important.

When Anger Becomes a Problem

Anger becomes a problem when it's not guided, or when it stays around too long. In the Ephesians passage just cited, Paul says we ought to deal right away with the issues that are stirring up the anger, rather than letting them linger, rather than ignoring them. *Don't let the sun go down on your anger.* It's not very likely you can actually stop the sun from setting, so I don't think that's what the apostle has in mind. It's better to look for constructive ways to respond to the situation causing the anger, and take appropriate actions that don't harm people, relationships, or things.

Referring back to the first *Biblical Principle of Marriage*, you always want to do what helps. It's usually not helpful to yell, scream, cuss, call names, insult, attack, hurt, accuse, blame, berate or talk bad about, have an affair, punish, avoid, ignore, repress, explode, give ultimatums, give the silent treatment, or pretend everything is okay.

Don't Do the Stupid Stuff

I call these behaviors *the Stupid Stuff*, because although they're natural and automatic responses to provocation, they never make the situation better. They're not smart and they don't help, so don't do the stupid stuff. Instead, here are some suggestions for responding to anger.

First, learn to slow down your anger. Your first impulses might not be helpful, but if you take a deep breath and then think about it a while, perhaps your subsequent behavior, instead of being destructive, will be helpful. As James 1:19 reminds us, *Everyone must be quick to hear, slow to speak, and slow to anger*. I find it interesting that his emphasis is on the speed of these behaviors.

The second step is to acknowledge your anger. When you're mad, admit it. Leo Madow's observation is that people like to think they're are governed by their intellect, but the truth is they're usually ruled by emotions. When the ruling emotion is anger, most people don't even know it, and the result may be violence, hostility, and destruction. Recognizing your anger, then, is an important step.

After that, identify the reason for your anger. This might take some time, but is crucial, because too often a husband or wife will lash out at the spouse over a trivial matter, when the real issue is a situation at your job that brought on the anger. Perhaps there's anger because of your finances, or a health issue. Unless you identify the reason for being angry, it's practically impossible to determine how best to direct your efforts at solving the problem. It's too easy to strike out at each other, even when the real problem lies elsewhere.

Then, you're ready to determine the intensity of the provocation and decide on an appropriate intensity of response. One couple who came for counseling had chronic anger, or as Gottman terms it, "a crabby habit of mind." The problem was that regardless of what they were unhappy about, they almost always responded with extreme rage. I explained what they were doing, and that not every circumstance called for an extreme response. There are big issues, and there are little issues, and they require different responses.

I asked them to make an Anger Chart, with ten anger levels, using a different word for each level of intensity. Then we talked about the responses that might be appropriate for each intensity level. Amazingly, it worked. Life took on a different, positive complexion for them. They learned how to tailor their responses to life's problems appropriately. An annoyance doesn't require rage. Nor does frustration. So, save the intensity for the truly big issues.

After you have identified the reason and the person you are angry with, talk to that person about it. This is the guidance given by Jesus in Matthew 18:15-17. The fact that you're angry is a sure sign that there is a problem to solve. The best course of action is to go and talk to the person involved. Many times, the problem can be cleared up, and reconciliation can occur right then and there.

Lastly, only fight once a week. Part of the problem in some marriages is that there's a fight every day. You never give each other time to recover and enjoy life. By limiting the fight to one day a week, you ensure an emotionally safe environment six days a week. And, when you're coming home from work, you know there won't be an argument tonight, because this isn't your *Fight Night*. This alone can make a difference in how you view being at home together.

Rules for Fight Night

1. Each person should bring up only one topic. The discussion will be limited to those two issues. Since your next fight will be the next week, you can bring up the next issues at that time.

2. You'll talk about a problem for only one hour. If it's not resolved, it'll be one of the problems next week.
3. Don't do the Stupid Stuff. Instead, choose words that will build each other up while moving towards a solution.
4. Work towards agreeing on a solution.
5. Write down your agreed-upon course of action in a journal. Remember, unity is built on agreements.
6. After two hours, *Fight Night* is over. Record any agreements you reached, close the book, get back to being friends until next week.

How to Apologize

It's a good thing to say you're sorry—but not just to avoid a fight. If there's genuinely something you've done that wasn't right, or if you hurt your mate, or if you haven't followed the rules for fighting, then it's appropriate and helpful to apologize. But when you say you're sorry, be specific about what you're apologizing for, and don't ever say, "I'm sorry, but." That's merely a lead-in to making an excuse or an accusation, or blaming your mate. "I'm sorry if" isn't much better. They don't help. And they might make the fight worse. Your mate might need to apologize also, but it's not your job to point that out. It's much better, honest, and helpful to say you're sorry for what you did, and leave it at that.

When you fight, it's important that you never do *the stupid stuff*. Never hit, kick, push, throw things, call names, insult, swear, cuss or yell. NEVER! NEVER! NEVER! This is not acceptable. EVER! Nobody should tolerate this kind of treatment or put up with it. Domestic violence is not part of the deal, not part of the agreement, not part of the marriage covenant.

You might have a hundred problems. So at your *Fight Night*, deal with the two biggest problems. Next week, you'll take on the next two biggest problems. After a couple months, you will agree on how to handle more than a dozen of your biggest problems. And when that happens, it's quite possible you won't need to continue having fight nights. You can turn them into *Date Nights*.

Yes, you get angry sometimes. That's normal. But what you do when you're angry is crucial to whether your marriage is going to last. When you start getting angry, you have to remind yourself to do the smart things instead of the stupid stuff. Slow down, lower your voice, back off, ask for clarification. Do not touch anyone when you are angry. Do not discipline your children when you are angry. Do not make love when you are angry. Because when you're angry you're too forceful, and out of control.

Talking Like Friends

This is the key. Friends talk together without criticizing or condemning each other. They're supportive and encouraging. They listen a lot. And they leave you with the feeling that you're glad you got together to talk. Married couples need to be able to do that, too.

PREP teaches the *Speaker/Listener Technique*. Gary Smalley called it *Drive-Through Talking*. Whenever you're trying to communicate and it's not going so well, it's time to use this method. Using this approach, you take turns talking without interrupting each other. After one of you speaks, the other will paraphrase what was just said, putting it into your own words. Then the original speaker will say "Yes, that's what I said," or "No, that's not what I meant." You'll repeat the process until you both understand what each other is saying.

This technique slows down the conversation, tones down the emotional intensity, helps you understand one another, and helps clarify what the real issue is. But it takes practice to get good at it.

Keep in mind, you're working towards a mutually satisfying solution. Sometimes this isn't possible, but it's worth the effort. If that doesn't solve the problem, ask for help. You might want to talk to a pastor or counselor. If the problem is at work, sometimes discussing it with your supervisor can help. The point is this: rather than letting anger go on and on, rather than taking it out on your family, rather than letting it eat at you and destroy you, the wise couple will work together to find solutions and making things better.

Even in great marriages there are situations where the husband and wife are upset with each other. That part is normal. What you do when you are angry with each other is what differentiates good marriages from not-so-great marriages. Anger that isn't handled well and in a timely manner can destroy your health, your relationships, your faith, and your career. Anger that is handled well results in solutions, and leads you back to happiness, peace, and contentment. It leads to a better relationship.

That's why God created human beings with the ability to communicate, and it's one of the aspects of being in the divine image. Now you're talkin'!

Now You're Talkin'

Discussion Starters

 Key Concept: Couples in a good marriage talk to maintain friendship, solve problems, and enhance romance.

 Discussion Points:

1. Do you have a story similar to *Her Diary, His Diary*? If so, was it funny or painful?
2. When do you and your spouse laugh together?
3. Which end of these spectrums do you and your spouse tend to be on?
   Report vs Rapport
   Fix-it vs Affirmation
   Hierarchy vs Community
4. Do you and your partner have any nonverbal signals or ways of communicating without words?

 Dig Deeper:

1. What words do you find affirming? What do you find discouraging?
2. What do you think about having a *Fight Night*? Do you think it might help?
3. Ask your partner to try the communication method called *Drive-through Talking* or *the Speaker Listener Technique*? How did it go? Most couples need to practice a few times before feeling like it's a natural way to discuss their issues.

TREASURE #4: FREEDOM

In Ephesians 5:21-25, marriage is said to be like our relationship with Christ. Since that is the case, we need to understand the impact Jesus has on us when he comes into our lives. A quick glance at Galatians 5:1 shows us what the Lord is up to in our lives: *Christ has liberated us to be free.*

Since husband and wife are called to represent the Lord to one another, the impact you have in each other's lives should be the same as what the Lord is doing. You are called to set each other free. Your love for each other and the way you treat each other should liberate each other, and remove constraints, yokes, or bondage. Love liberates you to pursue life, to fulfill dreams and aspirations, to live life to the fullest.

Jesus said, *I have come so that they may have life and have it in abundance.* Everyone who is married should be able to say this to his or her mate.

Does the way you and your spouse treat each other set you free? Free from fear or abuse? Free from a power struggle? Free from worry and stress? Free from debt? Free to relax and be yourself? Free to love and trust? Free to enjoy life and follow your dreams?

Does freedom adorn every room in your home? The *Biblical Principles of Marriage* will help you discover Treasure # 4.

TITLE DEED

You are not your own, for you were bought at a price. Therefore glorify God in your body.

1 Corinthians 6:19-20

A wife does not have the right over her own body, but her husband does. In the same way, a husband does not have the right over his own body, but his wife does.

1 Corinthians 7:4

The guy speaking at the annual educator's conference was eloquent, and better than most TED Talks. His message was cutting edge, funny, and he knew his stuff. It was obvious he had the audience in the palm of his hand. They loved his presentation, and they loved him. Plus, he was good-looking. He had everything going for him. It was a captivating presentation, and the attractive woman in the front row was smitten.

As soon as the speech was over, people from all over the auditorium came to the front to talk to him, ask a question, or to congratulate him for the powerful message he had given. She waited til everyone else was gone, and then said, "That was amazing. I'm staying here in the conference hotel. Would you like to stay with me tonight?"

Without hesitating, he looked at her and said, "That sounds like fun. My wife is right over here. Let me go ask her, and if she says it's OK, then sure, I'd love to." The look on her face changed, and she disappeared. That's not what she expected to hear.

Tenth Biblical Principle of Marriage:
You Are Not Your Own

The keynote speaker at the conference that night understood this concept. He knew who he belonged to, and who had authority over his body.

What the apostle Paul says to the Corinthian church in 1 Corinthians 6:18-20 is that your body doesn't belong to you. Your life doesn't belong to you. Jesus Christ bought and paid for you, and now you belong to him. The Lord owns you. Therefore, the way you live your life matters. You decided to live your life the way the Lord wants you to.

Then in chapter seven he writes, *A wife does not have the right over her own body, but her husband does. In the same way, a husband does not have the right over his own body, but his wife does.* In other words, you are not your own. You belong to Christ, who owns you. And if you're married, you are not your own, you belong to your spouse, who owns you. Therefore, you might consider your partner's preferences when trying to make lifestyle decisions.

I understand that this flies in the face of what the secular culture might be telling you. The message from your friends, your therapist, and the media may be more like, *Do your own thing. Who cares about what your partner says. Be your own person. Nobody owns you. If she doesn't like it, so what. If he doesn't like it, do it anyway. Be your own boss. You own yourself.* That's what a lot of voices might be telling you, but they're wrong . . . Every one of them.

Before you throw this book away, or decide that this concept is so outdated you're going to forget it and live the way you want to, please keep in mind that this is the Word of the Lord, that life works better this way, and marriage works better this way. But also, the harshness of being owned by someone is mitigated by the fact that ownership in marriage is mutual. You own each other. It's not a one-way street; it works both ways.

Body: Literal, Pronoun, and Metaphor

When the apostle Paul uses the word *body* in 1 Corinthians 7:4, *A wife does not have the right over her own body, but her husband does. In the same way, a husband does not have the right over his own body, but his wife does*, there are three ways to understand his meaning.

The literal way to read the verse is that it's talking about your physical body being owned by your spouse. In a literal sense, it's saying that your partner has the authority to make decisions that affect your body, because your body belongs to your spouse. Interestingly, this is what *a Medical Power of Attorney* establishes. In some states, it's called a *Power of Attorney for Healthcare*.

My wife and I have both a *Durable Power of Attorney* (financial/business authority) and a *Medical Power of Attorney* (medical/healthcare authority). You might consider preparing similar documents, but before you do, you need to make sure you have a relationship and a reputation of complete trust in each other.

A second way to read *body* in this verse is to see it as a pronoun. It can be interpreted to mean the self. A wife doesn't have authority over herself, nor does a husband have authority over himself. Biblical scholars point out that Paul sometimes uses *body* and *flesh* as if they were pronouns referring to the self. The apostle explains this in Ephesians 5:28, *In the same way, husbands are to love their wives as their own bodies. He who loves his wife loves himself.*

And a third way to understand *body* in 1 Corinthians 7 is as a metaphor for life. When I committed myself to Linda in marriage, I transferred ownership of my body, my self, and my entire life to her. When she married me, she made the same commitment.

That's why marriage can be scary. That's why the decision to marry shouldn't be made in a hurry, or before knowing each other pretty well. That's why Dr. John Van Epp teaches there are five ways of bonding with each other in a love relationship. Dr. Van Epp writes, *There is one basic rule for guarding the safe zone: never go further in one bonding area than you have gone in the previous.*

According to Van Epp, the five bonding areas are *Know, Trust, Rely, Commit,* and *Touch.* His research demonstrates that when a relationship progresses in this sequence of knowing and bonding, you maintain a certain amount of safety. This can keep you from making an unwise commitment or decision, so that by the time you marry and transfer ownership of your body, yourself, and your life, you can safely and confidently say you're in good hands.

Who Owns You

The context in 1 Corinthians chapters six and seven has to do with sexual morality. The reason why your personal lifestyle matters is because of who you belong to. If Christ owns you, then he calls the shots regarding your body, your self, and your life.

When you became a Christian, you acknowledged Jesus Christ as Lord and Master of your life: body, mind, and spirit. You yielded your will to his, which is the meaning of the old hymn *I Surrender All.* Recognizing Christ's ownership of your life isn't burdensome. It's an act of worship, because you literally become the temple of the Holy Spirit, who lives in you.

Similarly, when you marry, you turn your life over to your mate. It's not a matter of being dominated, it's a matter of mutual surrendering or yielding, because you love each other and are committed to what's best for one another. On the other hand, since your spouse owns you, you are no longer a free agent who can do anything that comes to mind. You are owned by your lover.

Years ago, we moved to a new town because of a new job. We were staying with my brother, and our stuff was still in the truck and in our car, waiting for us to move into an apartment. One morning after breakfast, I went outside to get in my car and go to work, but the car wasn't where I thought I parked it. So, I walked around, thinking I must have parked on the side street, but it wasn't there, either.

Practical Joke . . . Or Grand Theft Auto?

It suddenly dawned on me that my loving wife might have moved it. She is known to do practical jokes once in a while, but no, she insisted that she didn't move the car. That's when we realized it had been stolen. Parked right in front of the house, right at the end of the sidewalk. Somebody broke in and hotwired it while we were sleeping. If you ever had something taken, or worse, if you ever had someone break into your home, then you know the feeling of vulnerability I had that day.

I called the police to report the theft, and they found the car two days later. The car itself was fine, but they took everything inside the car: my tools and sports equipment. That's what hurt most. I don't think the police ever caught the guys who stole my car and the stuff in it.

The reason robbery is a crime is because our society understands *ownership*. The registration and the title of the car had

Linda's and my names on them. We had the right to determine who could use the car, and who couldn't.

Responsibility and Freedom

Similarly, when we bought a house, our names were on the contract, and on all the various forms we had to fill out. Those papers obligated us to pay for the house, but they also gave us permission to live there, watch TV there, have a dog, and decorate it however we want. We also have the authority to say who can come in, and who has to stay out. After living in apartments for years, it took a while before I stopped thinking I had to call the manager to get permission to paint the walls a different color. It's ours, and we can do whatever we want. But we have to take care of any repairs or problems that develop, unlike in a rental, where the owner or manager does a lot of the upkeep. Ownership means you have responsibilities, but also that you have a lot a freedom.

When you get married, it's like your spouse's name is printed on your heart. Guys, your wife owns you, and she is the one who has the authority to decide what you do with your body, your self, and your life. Ladies, your husband owns you, and he has authority to decide what you do with your body, your self, and your life.

What Ownership Doesn't Mean

The fact that your spouse owns you doesn't mean he or she makes all the decisions. It doesn't mean your mate can boss you around, bark out orders, or issue commands. It doesn't give your partner permission to abuse you or take advantage of you, and it doesn't mean you can't stand up for yourself.

What Ownership Does Mean

What it does mean is that you are accountable to each other. It means you are aware of each other's feelings, desires, and preferences, and you choose to honor one another with your body, your decisions, and your lifestyle.

Last night, my wife and I went out to dinner. While driving to the restaurant, I asked her what she thought about the biblical principle of mutual ownership. Her response surprised me, but I really like what she had to say.

It's like Jesus's parable about the Pearl of Great Price, she said. *The pearl was expensive. It cost the guy everything he had. But he was happy, because that pearl was precious to him. In the same way, marriage costs everything we have. But what we gain is precious.*

That's what a lot of people seem to overlook. Ownership implies that what you own is meaningful, valuable, and precious. You do whatever it takes to get it, and then you treasure it, and care for it because it's precious. Too many husbands and wives forget how precious their spouse is. How precious their marriage is. If it costs you everything, you can't afford to mess it up.

What You Don't Say – I Own You

The way I understand 1 Corinthians 7:4 is that it's never appropriate to say, "I own you." No, that's missing the point. Don't ever impose your ownership of your partner.

What You Do Say – You Own Me

Rather than saying "I own you," it's much more productive to say to your partner, "You own me." The intent of the scripture is to yield or surrender, not to usurp or demand. This leads to greater happiness, a more peaceful relationship, and a deeper understanding of what it means to be in love and in a committed relationship.

The context of Paul's discussion of ownership in 1 Corinthians 6 and 7 is about sexual morality, sexual freedom, and sexual fulfillment. The Corinthian Christians prided themselves on their ability to be spiritual, while at the same time flaunting their sexual freedom to have sex with whoever they wanted. Paul's response is that they don't understand ownership. Sexual promiscuity is wrong simply because Jesus owns you, and that kind of behavior doesn't represent him or his values. This is true for all Christians, whether married or single.

Sexual Morality for All Christians: Married or Single

1 Corinthians 7:1-2 teaches us to have nothing to do with *porneia*, which is the Greek word for sexual immorality of any kind. Do you remember this word from chapter five's discussion of Hebrews 13:4? *Porneia* includes unmarried sex, prostitution, having an affair, pornography, and a number of other sexual activities outside of marriage.

The topic shifts in 1 Corinthians 7:3. Because morality is important, if you want to be sexually active, you should get married, and limit your sexuality to your spouse. Furthermore, when you are married, part of your responsibility is to facilitate your partner's sexual fulfillment. And because your mate has authority over your body, don't withhold sex as a means of punishment or manipulation. That's not healthy for your relationship, nor is it biblical. If you're unhappy about something, there are positive and helpful ways to talk together and resolve the problem, but denying sex because you're upset isn't appropriate.

It's also not right to withhold sex because you think life without sex is more spiritual. Paul says abstaining from sex is okay for a short time when both partners agree, but not when your partner doesn't agree and not as a lifelong practice.

You belong to each other. You are both precious. Your marriage is precious. Protect it and nurture it. Just like your aim is to honor the Lord in every part of your life, your aim is to honor your spouse in every part of your life. This includes your sexuality.

Why Mutual Ownership is Good

As a couple, you have complete freedom to explore and experiment with sex and sensuality without guilt, without fear, and without shame. It's an important and healthy part of knowing each other and meeting each other's needs. It's important to cultivate a climate of safety, trust, confidence, and happiness. When you do this, sexual fulfillment is exciting and powerful.

Plus, this dynamic carries over to other aspects of your relationship because you're developing this freedom in a spirit of unity. Understanding who owns you and who you own, therefore, has to be included in a wholistic approach to your marriage.

If you are a married woman, your husband owns you, and has authority over your body, your self, and your life. If you are a married man, your wife owns you, and has authority over your body, your self, and your life. The passage in Corinthians is explicitly applied to both husband and wife, and is a clear statement of equality in marriage.

Talk about this with your mate. Explore the ways you can work this concept into your relationship. Reestablish the fact that you are both precious, and your marriage is precious. And treat each other accordingly.

I hope by now you're starting to see how the different *Biblical Principles of Marriage* fit together and overlap. By taking them all together in a comprehensive approach to growing your marriage, you can be the couple that lives happily ever after. Your dream of a lifetime of happiness together can come true.

Title Deed

Discussion Starters

 Key Concept: Your partner owns you. Therefore, make sure you honor your mate and your marriage by living to please your spouse.

 ### Discussion Points:

1. Other than your partner, what's something that you own that is precious to you?
2. Have you ever been robbed? If it's not too traumatic, are you willing to talk about what happened?
3. Has anyone ever told you that you should do your own thing regardless of how your spouse feels about it? What did you say?

 ### Dig Deeper:

1. How does it feel to think about being owned by your mate?
   How does it feel to be the owner of your spouse?
2. Is your marriage precious to you? Is your partner precious to you? How can you treat each other in ways that make you both feel special?

GIVE AND TAKE

. . . submitting to one another in the fear of Christ.

Ephesians 5:21

Eleventh Biblical Principle of Marriage:

Mutual Submission

Ephesians 5:21 provides the general guideline to submit to one another. This is how relationships work best, and this is the way the Kingdom of God operates. In 5:22-24 the principle is applied to wives. Then in 5:25, Paul tells husbands to *love your wives, just as Christ loved the church and gave himself up for her.*

Interestingly, the verb *submit* does not appear in the Greek text of Ephesians 5:22. It comes in the previous verse (5:21), which says, *Submit to one another as part of your reverence for Christ.* It is addressed to the whole congregation, and properly applies to all people in all relationships.

In other words, wives are to submit to their husbands, and husbands are to love their wives. Then, he defines love: it means to give yourself up for your spouse, like Jesus loved the church and gave up his life for his people. The point he's making is that loving and giving yourself up is the same as submission.

Therefore, Paul is really telling husbands and wives the same thing. *Wife, submit to your husband. And husband, submit to your wife.* This is what Jesus did for you, and this is how you should love the people in your life.

A lot of people mistakenly believe that the male is supposed to be in charge at all times, that the husband is always the boss, who not only gets to, but is supposed to, make all the decisions, and that the woman is the only one who has to submit. He can do whatever he wants, and she is supposed to stand there and take whatever he dishes out.

Many Christians think this is what the Bible teaches, but they're wrong. According to Gary Chapman, submission is meant to go both ways. Dr. Chapman's research agrees with the Bible, which teaches mutual submission. This is true for men and women. This is true for every relationship. And, it's true for marriage. Consider these statements from the New Testament One-Anothers that are directed toward all Christians.

- Wash one another's feet
- Honor one another
- Serve one another
- Carry each other's burdens
- Be humble toward one another
- Consider others better than yourselves
- Bear with one another
- Submit to one another

According to Ephesians chapter five, submission is not only for women; submission is not only for wives. It's always mutual. It always applies to men and women. Every follower of Christ is included, because that's the way Christians are commanded to live. When we live in mutual submission, the world is a better place, and relationships work better.

One-Sided Submission

I would go so far as to say this: many Christian men have been so adamant about demanding one-sided submission from their wife, that they stunted their own spiritual and psychological growth. By denying themselves the opportunity to practice the biblical command to submit, they haven't taken advantage of the opportunities to fully develop in character. In a good relationship, there's a healthy amount of give and take, a balance of giving in and having your way. This balance fosters maturity and completeness that are lacking otherwise.

The other side of the coin is that women who always submit may not be growing and developing as fully as they should, because they're not experiencing the full range of relational skills, either. The sad fact is that both husband and wife may be stilted in their maturation and growth because of the false teaching of one-sided submission. Some men in this scenario may feel just as trapped as the women. But they don't know how to break free, or they don't know they can.

One of the unfortunate side effects of this misunderstanding is many Christians don't have good marriages, and don't have an adequate understanding of what a good marriage can be. The Church has perpetuated a myth that is not based on the Bible or Christian values, but on ancient, pagan, pre-Christian culture and tradition, and this mistake has cost us dearly.

There are several reasons why this male-dominant, one-sided submission continues. First is the belief that "might makes right." Men are bigger and stronger, and therefore it makes sense that they are ordained by God to be in charge. Too many men use their strength and size to harm their family.

The belief that "might makes right," has been a source of abuse and violence throughout history, but the New Testament radically changes that. By teaching mutual submission, Paul says the strong should be just as submissive as those who are weak. Being bigger and stronger does not equate to the right to rule, dominate, or force one's will on others. That's just being a bully, and the Kingdom of God operates differently.

Kingdom Leadership

That's why Jesus contrasts Kingdom Leadership with the way leaders in the non-Christian sphere dominate and lord it over those they rule. The scriptures clearly teach a better use of power when it teaches that those who are strong have an obligation to help those who are weak. Those who are wealthy should share with those who are in need. Those who are healthy should care for those who are sick. And those who have knowledge should teach those who don't.

According to the Bible, the notion that "might makes right" is not true, and the concept of "divine right" is not compatible with the New Testament. Instead, the appropriate way for Christian men and women to think and act in relationship is mutual submission.

Another reason for the persistence of one-sided submission in marriage is cultural tradition. That's the way we've always done it. Besides, that's the way it is in many of the cultures around the world, so it must be right.

Culture versus God's Intent

To correct this, we have to understand the difference between traditional culture and authentic spirituality. The fact that the Old Testament people of God practiced a form of patriarchy doesn't imply that the Lord wanted them to do that. God chose to interact with humanity through their preexisting culture. He blessed them and loved them, even though they had flaws and misunderstandings, just like he does with you and me.

But the plan of God all along was to move humans away from that kind of lop-sided understanding of power and control in relationship, to a true equality. That's why on page one in your Bible, men and women were created in God's image, men and women given the instruction to rule the earth and have dominion. We'll take a deeper look at this in the last chapter of the book.

Paul writes in Galatians 3:24-25, *The law, then, was our guardian until Christ, so that we could be justified by faith. But since that faith has come, we are no longer under a guardian.* The Lord started working with fallen human beings at a certain point in history, gradually bringing us closer to what he really wanted our lives and culture to be like, restoring us to what he created us to be at the start. And now that the Messiah has come and his spirit lives in us, according to Galatians 3:29, in Christ *there is no Jew or Greek, slave or free, male or female; for you are all one in Christ Jesus.* In Jesus Christ, men and women are restored to complete equality, and this includes those who are married.

A third factor is the destructive role models many have seen in the marriages of their parents, other friends and family, and church leaders. Too many people grew up with terrible examples of couples who modeled relationship styles that were less than ideal, with incorrect communication and behavior patterns. Unfortunately, since they've never seen it done right, the misunderstanding persists.

The world needs to see Christian couples who are in love, who treat each other right, who model godliness and spirituality, who at the same time, set an example of what it means to live *WisdomBuilt* lives. The church needs to see this, too.

After studying the Bible, after examining a large amount of research from marriage experts, and after more than forty years of marriage and pastoral experience, I've concluded that the typical model of one-sided submission never was God's plan. And it never helped a couple achieve the kind of marriage the Lord wants them to have.

Mutual Submission is God's Idea

Submitting to one another in the fear of Christ is addressed to the whole congregation, and properly applies to all people in all relationships. The context for the remainder of Ephesians chapter five and the first nine verses of chapter six is the mutual submission explicitly stated in 5:21. The apostle applies the principle of mutual submission to three sets of relationship pairs: husband-wife (5:22-33), parent-child (6:1-4), and master-slave (6:5-9).

John Piper says it this way. *In other words, submit to each other…in Ephesians 5, submission is a wider Christian virtue for all of us to pursue, and it has its unique and fitting expressions in various relationships.*

Yes, wives are to be submissive to their husbands, but husbands are also to be submissive to their wives. Yes, children are to be submissive to their parents, but parents are also to be submissive to their children. Yes, slaves are to be submissive to their masters, but masters are also to be submissive to their slaves. This is why the apostle's message is revolutionary.

Referring back to Ephesians 5:21, the apostolic teaching is that because of our reverence for the Lord Jesus Christ, we are to honor all people, for all are created in the Image of God, the *Imago Dei*. We will have a submissive, humble approach in all of our relationships. And we'll apply this to family life as well as public life.

The same concept is seen in Philemon, Paul's letter to the Christian slave owner whose slave had run away. When

Onesimus the slave became a Christian, the apostle sent him back to Philemon, urging Philemon to consider him not only as a slave, but as a fellow human being, and as a dear brother.

James 1:27 reminds us that *Pure and undefiled religion before our God and Father is this: to look after orphans and widows in their distress and to keep oneself unstained by the world.* This is another way of saying that how we talk and act, and how we treat those who are weaker or needier, are evidence of whether we have been polluted by the world, or whether we have been shaped by the Spirit of God.

Christian men are called by God to use their strength to help, to protect, and to love. Husbands are called to submit to their wives just as certainly as wives are called to submit to their husbands.

What Submission Looks Like

There are many ways this can be implemented in a marriage. How might this impact the decision-making process, for example? Some couples take turns making decisions. Others make every decision together, talking it out until they agree on what to do. One method is to have the partner who is more knowledgeable in that area make the decision. Another possibility would be for the partner who feels more passionate on that issue to decide. My wife and I have used every one of these methods. The key is to build and maintain unity in the marriage, to honor one another, and foster equality and mutuality.

Another way mutual submission might show up in marriage is the way you balance two careers. We decided early on that a wife's career is just as important as a husband's. We also realized, that it's sometimes difficult for both to get good jobs in the same area at the same time. Because of this, my wife and I have taken turns making professional sacrifices in order to further the other's career.

A few years ago, I was pastoring a good church when my wife had an opportunity to join the faculty at a university that was a bit too far to commute. After discussing it, praying about it, and thinking it through, I decided to resign from the ministry position in order for her to take the teaching job. A lot of people criticized me for doing that, because they believed the husband and his career mattered, and the wife and her interests should always be subservient or marginalized. A few months after we moved, the Lord opened the doors to another ministry opportunity for me. Linda found fulfillment in her career, and so did I.

Ten years later, I had a chance to go into the Army as an Active Duty Chaplain. Knowing how much that meant to me, Linda willingly resigned from the teaching position that she loved, in order to facilitate my dream of being a military chaplain. It just so happened, that my first duty station was near a university that had a PhD program in her field. She applied and was accepted.

As she was completing her degree, she got a new job that wouldn't have been possible had she not completed the doctorate. Again, one of us submitted so the other could pursue a career opportunity. Every time we did that, it worked out to the benefit of the one who was making the sacrifice, and we were both able to pursue our dreams.

We've seen mutual submission work in big ways and small, once-in-a-lifetime events and everyday situations: giving in to each other, doing a favor, taking a back seat while the other has an opportunity for advancement, helping with chores around the house, or choosing the movie the other wants to see. It all adds up.

Perhaps another key verse to consider in this discussion is from Philippians 2:3-4, *Do nothing out of rivalry or conceit, but in humility consider others as more important than yourselves. Everyone should look out not only for his own interests, but also for the interests of others.*

Consider others as more important than yourself? That's not what a lot of voices are telling you these days, but that's the point of mutual submission: thinking, behaving, and living each day as if your spouse matters more, is more important. In the process, you get to watch your partner and your marriage flourish.

Linda and I have practiced mutual submission for more than forty years, and it continues to be a major factor in the success of our marriage. In essence, by practicing mutual submission, you are investing in your mate, your marriage, and yourself, and that investment pays huge dividends.

The Proverbs 31 Man

Take a fresh look at Proverbs 31 and the person we know as *the Proverbs 31 Woman*. She is smart and aggressive. She's ambitious and makes decisions. She and her husband trust each other. She's an entrepreneur, yet she gives to the needy. She has no fear. She supports her husband and his concerns, and he is just as supportive of her and her interests. She is a model of success in business and in the community. She teaches others with wisdom and skill, and at the same time manages her household. Her sons and her husband respect her, praise her, and admire her. In fact, the whole community sees her as a leader.

Maybe we need to focus on the *Proverbs 31 Man*. He is supportive. He listens to his wife. He praises her and encourages her. He recognizes her authority and influence publicly and in the home. He never undermines her or tells her to take a back seat. He values her strengths, and all she has to offer him, their family, and their community. And he wants her to reach her full potential in every arena.

Ladies and gentlemen, this is a picture of mutual submission. But more than mutual submission, it's mutual encouragement. You are each other's best cheerleaders. You never try to hold each other back. Remember, you win or lose as a team. And you can both be all-stars.

Strength, Wisdom, and Maturity

Submission doesn't deny headship. Nor does it imply weakness. Ephesians 5:21 begins with *Submit to one another*. The next section begins in 6:10, *Finally, be strengthened by the Lord and by His vast strength*. It's clear that submission and strength don't cancel each other out. Instead, they complement each other.

For a man to submit to his wife is not a sign of weakness, but an indication of strength, wisdom, and maturity. For a woman to submit to her husband doesn't mean she has no identity. It's an indication of strength, wisdom, and maturity. It's the same for husband and wife.

Couples who submit to each other will have a stronger, happier marriage. They will be able to withstand the attacks of the enemy. They'll be able to overcome temptation, hardship, and other pitfalls of married life. They'll pray for each other. They'll have what it takes to persevere and endure. In other words, they'll reach both of the goals we stated at the start of this book: they'll be happy, and their marriage will last a lifetime.

In Genesis, when God created male and female in his image, he intended them to experience equality, unity, and intimacy. These ideals were marred by sin. In Christ, however, and by the presence of the Holy Spirit in your lives, the Lord wants to restore you to the kind of marriage he had in mind from the start.

Let's Start a New Culture & Tradition

What we need among Christian couples is to correct the misunderstandings about one-sided submission by starting a new tradition and a new culture – not just doing it differently, but doing it right. This is why God became incarnate, this is why the Holy Spirit was given to the Church, and this is why we have the Bible: that we'd be transformed to a new way of thinking.

We are talking about a whole new way of looking at marriage. Mutual submission, accompanied by Jesus's style of leadership in the home, can usher in a revolutionary approach to relationship that is thoroughly biblical, yet completely practical.

The beauty of properly understanding mutual ownership and mutual submission is the awesome freedom that comes into the relationship. Neither of you has to pretend to have it all together, because you're sharing the responsibilities. There's no coercion to play along with preestablished gender roles because you're free to define your relationship according to the *Biblical Principles of Marriage*, and what works for you. There's no more fight in the marriage. Instead, you're liberated to focus on serving one another, helping each other fulfill lifelong dreams, and building the kind of marriage you really want

WisdomBuilt Biblical Principles of Marriage

Discussion Starters

 Key Concept: Mutual submission is necessary in building a great marriage, and was God's plan from the day he created man and woman.

 Discussion Points:

1. Can you think of someone in your childhood, teens, or early adulthood who encouraged you?
2. How does it feel when someone takes you and your opinions seriously?
3. In what ways have you and your partner submitted to one another?

 Dig Deeper:

1. What dynamics do you see in the Proverbs 31 couple? Do you and your partner share those traits?
2. What would complete freedom to be who you want to be and do what you want to do look like? What would it feel like?
3. Talk with your mate about the dynamics in your relationship. Are there any changes you think might make things better? Are there changes your partner might like to see?

IMAGO DEI

So God created man in His own image; He created him in the image of God; He created them male and female. God blessed them, and God said to them, "Be fruitful, multiply, fill the earth, and subdue it. Rule the fish of the sea, the birds of the sky, and every creature that crawls on the earth."

Genesis 1:27-28

Gender equality was supposed to be established 3,000 years ago. Unfortunately, the Old Testament people of God didn't pick up on it, and the New Testament people of God haven't done much better.

The concept that people bear the divine image wasn't new. When the creation story in Genesis was written, many cultures believed their leader to be a son of god or a representative of god. Ancient civilizations in Asia, Africa, Europe, and the Americas held similar beliefs.

The biblical creation story is radically different, though. Many religions believed only their leader had the divine image, and their ruler was almost always an upper-class man of the dominant ethnicity.

The Bible is Revolutionary and Radical

Genesis comes along and says something revolutionary. Every human being is created in God's image. This includes women, people from all ethnic groups, and commoners. That's what makes the religion of the Bible radically different from most other religions of the world.

Right from the start, God decided there would be total equality. All human beings were to be treated fairly with equal opportunities, there being no glass ceiling or any kind of artificial limitations that restrict people groups who are less favored. There was to be no hate, no fear, and no bias. Nobody was to be superior or inferior to others.

Though the majority of cultures around the world have had some form of caste system that subjugated women, minorities, children, and the less fortunate, the plan of God was to move humans away from that kind of thinking about society and relationships. That's why page one in your Bible says men and women were created in God's image, and men and women were given the instruction to rule the earth and have dominion.

God's Image Equally in Men and Women

Genesis is specific and clear. Men and women are equally created in God's image. Men and women are equally given the command to rule and subdue the earth. According to Old Testament scholars, the creation narrative uses the Language of Royalty, the Language of Authority, the Language of Relationship, and the Language of Equality.

- Royalty: all people are considered royalty and treated accordingly.
- Authority: all human beings are given authority to rule and subdue the earth.
- Relationship: everyone has the divine image and can be in relationship with God.
- Equality: all people are created in God's image, and have equal worth and standing.

Imago Dei

The biblical account of creation makes it clear that though we were made in the image of God, we are not deity. By specifying that we are *in his likeness*, it's saying we are like god, we represent god, and we are in relationship with god, but God is God and we are not. These facts have some far-reaching implications about how we treat people, including how couples treat each other.

Being in God's image and likeness is an important part of the Judeo-Christian world view. We're not merely the product of a godless evolutionary process. While we may have many similarities with the animals, what distinguishes humans from the rest of creation is the image of God, which is a major theme discussed by theologians. The Latin term for Image of God is *Imago Dei*.

The *Westminster Shorter Catechism* summarizes the doctrine of man created in the image of God like this: "How did God create man? God created man male and female after his own image, in knowledge, righteousness, and holiness, with dominion over the creatures."

You Are Like God and You Represent God

To be in God's image and likeness has two meanings. First, it means we are like God in some significant ways. Second, it means we represent him in some important ways.

How we are *like* God refers to his activity and character and the ways we are like him. God communicates. He creates. He relates. He loves. He keeps his word. He is loyal. He is compassionate. He cares. He has knowledge. We can make these same statements of human beings, because we are fashioned in his image. We have the ability to create, to communicate, to relate, and to love. We too have moral capabilities such as loyalty and honesty. We have an ability to show compassion and care. We have the capacity for knowledge. In that we are like our creator, we have the ability to make our world a better place for ourselves and for the people in our lives.

For over a year, I drove more than fifty miles to work each day, and then the same distance home in the evening. The traffic on the freeway was often pretty bad, usually rainy, and as you've probably experienced a time or two, other drivers are sometimes not very nice. During that experience, I started despising those drivers who made stupid decisions on the road, and I developed a bad attitude. I started noticing my attitude problem after a few months and realized I needed to do something to correct it.

After praying about it several times, I decided to come up with something I could say out loud whenever another driver irked me. Here's what I wrote.

You are a fabulous human being, fashioned in the indelible image of the Creator.

After I memorized it, I started reciting it out loud in my car whenever I saw a driver do something dumb or dangerous. Sometimes ten, fifteen, twenty times a day. Nobody else knew what I was doing. I'm the only one who heard me, even though I actually said it loudly at times. It helped me remember that every man and every woman has the divine image, even those who are not living for the Lord. Even those who are terrible drivers.

The concept of representing God has a different focus. There's a different starting point for how we think and how we live. From this perspective, the emphasis is not on how we are like God, but that we represent the Lord to the world. We represent God and his values to the planet and to other people. We represent him in matters of social justice and spirituality. This is one of the reasons Christians should be involved in the community, why we should set an example of alleviating pain in the world, and caring for the needy.

The idea that God's people represent him to the world continues in the New Testament. Paul reaffirms this theme in 2 Corinthians 5:20 when he writes, *Therefore, we are ambassadors for Christ*. Now, not only do we have the divine image, we also have the Holy Spirit in us, another powerful reason for understanding we are to represent the Lord at all time and in all circumstances.

Then in Galatians 3:28 he says, *There is no Jew or gentile, slave or free, male or female. You are all the same in Christ.* The apostle emphasizes total equality in Christ and in the Church. The gospel of Jesus Christ comes to eradicate social injustice of every kind, and the followers of Christ are his agents of change in the world.

Those changes have to begin at home. Christians should be leading the way when it comes to fighting for racial harmony and justice, gender equality, caring for the poor, and many other societal challenges. Whatever impact the Lord would have if he were present is the impact the church should have because we are Christ in the world.

Twelfth Biblical Principle of Marriage: Husband and Wife in the Image of God

The application of this concept in marriage is the mutual recognition that both husband and wife are made in the image of God. In a very real way, you have to look at your mate and see the face of God. How you treat your partner is how you're treating God himself.

Jesus taught his followers that when they gave a cup of water to someone who was thirsty, or when they did any act of kindness for another person, it was as if they were doing it for the Lord himself. The same is true today. There is an obligation and an opportunity to honor the image of God by honoring one another.

This is why the apostle Peter urges husbands to treat their wives with honor and respect. Plus, their prayers may be hindered if they dishonor the image (1 Peter 3:7). Similarly, in Ephesians 5:33 Paul tells wives to treat their husbands with respect. It goes both ways.

Not only do you treat each other well because of the image of God in your spouse, but because you represent God to each other. God is a God of graciousness, mercy, love and kindness. He comes into your life to encourage, inspire, and bring hope and strength. In other words, the Lord comes into your life to make things better. That's the same kind of impact you can have on your partner.

A few years ago, my wife mentioned some honey-do chores around the house that she wanted me to take care of. I told her I would do them, but after several weeks the tasks were still not done. Linda was frustrated, but she never nagged, never yelled. She reminded me every once in a while, but mostly remained patient and understanding. She never got angry and never punished me. I learned a lot about the patience and graciousness of the Lord by watching how she handled the situation.

You can probably tell by know that I had to learn some of these principles the hard way. I'm still not perfect by any means. The fact is, you don't have to be perfect. The point is to keep growing, continue helping each other, serving one another, and submitting to each other. As you do these things, you and your partner will grow and experience the blessings of the Lord. You'll decorate your home with beautiful treasures. You'll build an attractive, happy home together.

Imago Dei

Make the World a Better Place

Edward Bok was a Dutch immigrant to the United States, a Pulitzer Prize-winning author, Christian, and world peace advocate. His personal guiding principle in life, and his message to others, was to make the world a "bit better or more beautiful because you have lived in it." These were the words of Mr. Bok's Christian grandmother, and he adopted them as his own philosophy of life.

This might be a good motto for Christian couples to consider today – to make life better in some way for each other every day. My goal is to make the world a bit better or more beautiful for my wife because I am her husband, a bit better for my sons because I am their father, even though they are grown and have families of their own.

It would be worth brainstorming about the ways you are like God, and just as helpful to talk together about how you are called to represent him. Both are powerful concepts, full of meaning for you as an individual, and for you as a couple. It's also helpful to take a fresh look at Jesus once in a while because he dealt with some of the same issues when he encountered people.

Show Me the Money

Some men tried to get Jesus in trouble one day by asking him a trick question. *Is it right to pay taxes to Caesar?* It was a well-thought-out trap. If he said *No*, then he'd be in trouble with the Roman authorities, and if he said *Yes*, the Jewish religious leaders would be upset with him and declare him to be an ungodly, unrighteous man because they felt it was wrong to pay tribute to the pagan emperor. But Jesus had an interesting reply.

Show Me the coin used for the tax." So they brought Him a denarius. *"Whose image and inscription is this?" He asked them.*

"Caesar's," they said to Him. *Then He said to them, "Therefore give back to Caesar the things that are Caesar's, and to God the things that are God's"* (Matthew 22:19-22).

The guys who tried to trip him up didn't know what to do next. They were stunned by his answer, and walked away shaking their heads.

The answer Jesus gave was significant on three levels. On the surface, he avoided their trap by simply saying give to each person what's already his. It's Caesar's money. It has his name and picture on it. So, give Caesar his denarius. He sidestepped their trap.

There's a deeper meaning to his answer, however. The verb give that Jesus uses here literally means to give back. The money is Caesar's, who loaned it to you. Now give it back to him. Then Jesus adds, *And give back to God the things that are God's.* You belong to God, who loaned your life to you, now give yourself back to him. This is a direct reference to the creation story in Genesis chapter one, which says human beings were created in the image of God.

Jesus is telling the Jewish people that they had stopped acting like they were God's people. He's reminding them that all human beings have the divine image, and therefore belong to God, who owns them. Because people carry the image of God, all people are called to live in integrity, purity, and justice, representing God in all they do.

Plus, there's a subtle third message in Jesus's reply that we can't afford to miss. The coin was most likely a denarius featuring the image of Tiberius. In Latin, the inscription on the front says, *Caesar Augustus Tiberius, son of the Divine Augustus,* and the reverse says *Highest Priest.* Caesar claimed to be the son of god and the high priest. These are the very claims Jesus made about himself: Son of God, and High Priest.

The image and message on the Roman coin were indeed sacrilegious, because the Romans practiced Caesar-worship. On the other hand, the image and message of the true God is on every human being. You belong to God. Therefore, give back to the Lord what is his.

You Belong to God

Whether you are male or female, because you are made in the image of God, there's nobody in the world more important or more valuable than you. At the same time, there's nobody lower than you or less important. You are free to be yourself, free to pursue your dreams, and free to express yourself, and in that freedom, you can liberate others to do the same, starting with your partner, extending to your children, reaching out to your neighbor, your church, and your community.

When you and your spouse are free to be all God wants you to be, your life will take on so much joy, fulfillment, and excitement that you won't be able to contain it. It'll radiate from you, drawing people like a magnet, changing your marriage, and impacting your world.

Discussion Starters

Key Concept: All humans are created in God's image: people of all gender, ethnicity, nationality, and caste.

Discussion Points:

1. In your opinion, what is the image of God?
2. Are men and women supposed to be equal in the home? In the church? In the workplace?
3. Where have you seen unfairness or injustice?
4. How does your spouse make life better for you?

Dig Deeper:

1. In what ways do you see the Imago Dei in your spouse?
2. Are there any aspects of character that you would like to become more like Christ?

3. In what ways do you think Galatians 3:28 should be understood spiritually and how could it be understood practically?
4. What can you do as a couple to make your world a bit better or more beautiful?

ATMOSPHERE/CLIMATE

He got up, rebuked the wind, and said to the sea, "Silence! Be still!" The wind ceased, and there was a great calm.

Mark 4:39

Because my wife and I have family living in different states and overseas, my wife sets her phone to show the weather in quite a few places. She'll often tell me who in the family has the hottest or coldest temperature of the day and where it's raining or snowing. She says it helps her feel more connected to family members who are far away.

She also likes to know details about weather that make no sense to me. For example, it might be 85 degrees, but her phone adds that it "feels like" 92. My typical response is something like, "What do you mean *feels like*? If it's 85 degrees, it feels like 85 degrees, cause that's what 85 feels like in these conditions." That's when she'll roll her eyes and shake her head at me. Obviously, it makes sense to her . . . and to whoever came up with a way to measure what it *feels like*. But it makes no sense to me.

What does make sense to me is if it's going to rain, I need an umbrella. We used to live where it snowed, and when there was snow or ice on the roads, I needed to make sure the chains were in the trunk. If it was cold outside, I needed a jacket or sweater, because being prepared for the weather is important.

The largest building in the world is the Boeing plant in Everett, Washington. It's large enough for Disneyland to fit completely inside. It can hold twelve Empire State Buildings, or you could put seventy-five football fields inside. However you want to measure, it's huge, so big that it has its own weather. Workers have seen clouds and rainbows inside the building. There have even been reports of rain. Boeing engineers had to install expensive climate control mechanisms, the main concerns being humidity and temperature.

Even regular-size buildings and homes need climate control. Smaller buildings might not have clouds and rainbows and rain, but temperature and humidity can make a big difference when it comes to comfort, enjoyment, and quality of life. We tend to heat our buildings when it's cold, and turn on the air conditioner when it's hot. Or at least have a fan blowing. We use a humidifier to add moisture to the air, and a dehumidifier to remove moisture. We have filters to control dust and allergens, and pesticide services to take care of the bugs. We want the environment to be just right for us, our kids, and our guests.

What's the Climate in Your Home?

A lot of people fail to recognize that the emotional environment is just as important as the meteorological factors. In fact, it's more important. They'll spend a lot of money on the comfort of the home, but do nothing to maintain the right emotional climate. They'll do everything possible to make everyone comfortable physically, while at the same time maintaining an environment that is toxic emotionally or spiritually.

Using the analogy of the *feels like* feature of my wife's weather app, what does it feel like to be in your home? When you, your partner, your kids, or your guests walk into your house, what do

Atmosphere / Climate

they sense? What do they feel? Or to put it another way, what kind of air do they breathe?

In early 2017, a family in Amarillo, Texas, got sick. By the time someone called the paramedics, one child was already unconscious. First responders couldn't revive the child. Six other family members were taken to the hospital, where three more children died. An investigation concluded that someone had used a pesticide that emitted a strong odor. When the family tried to wash it away by hosing the area with water, the chemical combined with the water to create a toxic, lethal gas that caused cardiac arrest. Simply being in the house and breathing the air, sickened the family, and killed four children.

In March of 2018, a family from Iowa went to a vacation condo, not knowing there was an odorless, toxic gas in the building. All four of them died: mom, dad, two kids.

That's exactly what a lot of people are doing to their families emotionally. They focus on the house, the toys, the furnishings, the appearances, and all the while, they're killing each other with their words, attitudes, and actions. Visitors come and go, some of them realizing what's happening, but most seem not to notice, because they too live in a toxic environment.

When people walk into your home, what do they see and hear? What do they feel and taste? What do they smell and what do they breathe? Is the emotional experience in your home healthy and life-giving, or is it toxic, slowly eating away at your happiness and health? Is the environment pleasant, making people feel comfortable and at ease? Or does it put people on edge, like walking on egg shells, having to be on their guard? Can you smell fear? Is there a sense of awkwardness? Do you feel uneasy or unsafe?

In some marriages, the climate is sunny and warm, with a gentle breeze that brings a smile to the face and the soul. In others, there's always a storm brewing, fierce winds blowing, with thunder and lightning. Some have fresh air, while others are filled with dangerous levels of smog. Which of these atmospheres do you have in your home?

When we lived in the Los Angeles area, one of the daily news features was the air quality report. Smog alerts were common. When the smog got so bad that it was dangerous to exercise or even be outside, the newscasters would make sure we knew about it.

When I was in the Army, every once in a while, we had to complete the chemical warfare training, which meant a trip to the gas chamber. The chem suit had boots, gloves, pants, jacket, and protective mask, all designed to prevent airborne gas from touching the skin or being inhaled. We put the suit on outside, then about a dozen of us at a time went inside the chamber.

When the NCO gave the order, we took off the protective mask, and had to stay long enough that we couldn't hold our breath anymore. As soon as we breathed, our lungs, sinuses, nose, and eyes hurt and stung. It was horrible. Tough men and women started throwing up or gagging. The experience was necessary, however, because we needed to know how to use the protective equipment and to trust it, in case we ever found ourselves in a situation where chemical warfare was a real threat.

Do the people in your life feel like they have to wear a chem suit with protective mask whenever they enter your house? Or do they know they can breathe easy, because it's a safe place?

The sensations that you and your guests experience in your home are determined by the way you treat each other in the marriage and in the family. Therefore, you need to be intentional

Atmosphere / Climate

about the experience you want the people in your home to have. What do your children and your guests experience when they're around you? Is the atmosphere pleasant? Is the air safe to breathe? Is it a good environment?

When taken together, the *Biblical Principles of Marriage* will foster a climate and a context for creating unity, emotional safety, and peace. You can establish an atmosphere of love that is noticeable to everyone who enters your home. The way you and your spouse think about each other, talk to and about each other, and treat each other are crucial to your emotional health and safety, for your children, and for anyone else who interacts with you.

In Mark chapter four, Jesus and his disciples were in a boat on the Sea of Galilee, when a powerful storm started up. Most of the men in the boat were terrified, but Jesus simply got up, rebuked the wind, and said to the sea, *"Silence! Be still!" The wind ceased, and there was a great calm.*

If your home is like a storm, and the people in your family are afraid, you, too, can call on the Lord. He can calm the storm in your life, just like he did in the boat with his disciples. If your marriage has been a battle zone, it may be time to take your spouse out to dinner and call a truce. Make a plan to start creating a peaceful, life-giving atmosphere and decorating your marriage with precious and beautiful treasures.

It will take a little time and effort, but you really can be the couple who has a marriage built on the right foundation. There's never a better time to start than right now.

IF YOU WANT MORE

I hope you enjoyed reading *WisdomBuilt Biblical Principles of Marriage*. If you want more helpful information about marriage, you're welcome to take a look at my website, paullinzey.com. You may use the contact page to ask a question, tell me what you think of the concepts in the book, or to request my monthly newsletter. Also, if your church, fellowship group, or organization would like me to speak at an event, please let me know. I'd love to hear from you.

www.paullinzey.com

NEW TESTAMENT ONE ANOTHERS

Love one another, for love comes from God. Everyone who loves has been born of God and knows God.

1st John 4:7-8

John 13:14	Wash one another's feet
John 13:34	Love one another
Romans 2:1	Don't judge one another
Romans 12:10	Be devoted to one another
Romans 12:10	Honor one another
Romans 12:16	Be in agreement with each other
Romans 14:13	Don't criticize each other
Romans 14:19	Build each other up
Romans 15:5	Live in harmony with each other
Romans 15:7	Accept one another
Romans 15:14	Teach each other
Romans 16:16	Greet one another with a holy kiss
1 Corinthians 11:33	Wait for one another
1 Corinthians 12:25	Be concerned for each other
Galatians 5:13	Serve one another
Galatians 5:15	Don't bite and devour each other
Galatians 5:26	Don't envy one another
Galatians 6:2	Carry each other's burdens
Ephesians 4:32	Be kind & compassionate to one another
Ephesians 4:32	Forgive each other
Ephesians 5:19	Speak to each other in psalms, hymns, and spiritual songs

WisdomBuilt Biblical Principles of Marriage

Ephesians 5:21	Submit to one another
Philippians 2:3	Consider others better than yourselves
Colossians 3:9	Don't lie to each other
Colossians 3:13	Bear with one another
1 Thessalonians 4:18	Encourage each other
1 Thessalonians 5:11	Build each other up
1 Thessalonians 5:13	Live in peace with each other
1 Thessalonians 5:15	Pursue what is good for one another
Hebrews 10:24	Spur one another on toward love and good works
James 5:9	Don't complain about each other
James 5:16	Pray for each other
James 5:16	Confess your sins to one another
1 Peter 4:9	Be hospitable to one another
1 Peter 5:5	Humility toward one another
1 John 1:7	Fellowship with one another

BIBLICAL PRINCIPLES OF MARRIAGE

A house is built by wisdom, and it is established by understanding;

by knowledge the rooms are filled with every precious and beautiful treasure.

Proverbs 24:3-4

Principles	Chapter	Chapter Titles
Designed to Help	1	Sidekicks
Let Go of the Past	2	Baggage
Created for Unity	3	On the Same Team
The Gift of Spirituality	4	Heaven on Earth
Sex & Sensuality	5	Sex & Sensuality
Having Fun Together	6	Are We Having Fun Yet
Knowing Each Other	7	Yada, Yada, Yada
Words Are Powerful	8	Now You're Talkin'
Friendship	9	You've Got a Friend in Me
You Are Not Your Own	10	Title Deed
Mutual Submission	11	Give and Take
In the Image of God	12	Imago Dei

BIBLIOGRAPHY

Arthur, Kay. A Marriage Without Regrets. Eugene, OR: Harvest House, 2000.

Augustine, Sue. When Your Past is Hurting Your Present. Eugene, OR: Harvest House, 2005.

Benner, David. Strategic Pastoral Counseling. Grand Rapids: Baker Academic, 2003.

Berger, Lauren, et al. "Friendship." Encyclopedia Britannica. 26 January 2017. https://www.britannica.com/topic/friendship. Accessed November 9, 2018.

Child, Lee. *Killing Floor*. New York: Jove Books, 1997.

Chapman, Gary. Now You're Speaking My Language. Nashville: B&H Books, 2007.

Chapman, Gary. The 5 Love Languages. Chicago: Northfield Publishing, 2010.

Chapman, Gary. The Marriage You've Always Wanted. Chicago: Moody Publishers, 2005.

Cloud, Henry. Changes that Heal. Grand Rapids: Zondervan, 1992.

Cloud, Henry and John Townsend. How to Have That Difficult Conversation You've Been Avoiding. Grand Rapids: Zondervan, 2005.

Driscoll, Mark and Grace. Real Marriage: The Truth About Sex, Friendship & Life Together. Nashville: Thomas Nelson, 2011.

Evans, Tony. Marriage Matters. Chicago: Moody Publishers, 2010.

George, Jim. A Husband After God's Own Heart. Eugene: Harvest House, 2004.

Gill, Deborah M. and Barbara Cavaness, God's Women Then and Now. Springfield, MO: Grace & Truth, 2004.

Gottman, John M., et al. The Relationship Cure. New York: Three Rivers Press, 2001.

Gottman, John M., et al. 10 Lessons to Transform Your Marriage. New York: Three Rivers Press, 2006.

Gottman, John and Nan Silver. The Seven Principles for Making Marriage Work. New York: Three Rivers Press, 1999.

Harley, Willard F. Jr. Effective Marriage Counseling. Grand Rapids: Revell, 2010.

Jeremiah, David. What the Bible Says about Love, Marriage, & Sex. New York: Faith Words, 2012.

Keller, Timothy. The Meaning of Marriage. New York: Dutton, 2011.

Kendrick, Stephen and Alex Kendrick. The Love Dare. Nashville: B&H Publishing, 2008.

Kotter, John P. Leading Change. Boston: Harvard Business Review Press, 2012.

Markman, Howard J., et al. Fighting for Your Marriage. San Francisco: Jossey-Bass, 2001.

Markman, Howard J., et al. 12 Hours to a Great Marriage. San Francisco: Jossey-Bass, 2004.

Mason, John. Let Go of Whatever Holds You Back. Grand Rapids: Revell, 2012.

McGraw, Phillip C. Relationship Rescue. New York: Hyperion, 2000.

Parrot, Les and Leslie Parrot. Your Time-Starved Marriage. Grand Rapids: Zondervan, 2006.

Piper, John. This Momentary Marriage. Wheaton: Crossway Books, 2009.

Reachout. "What is Friendship?" Reachout.com: Helping You Get Through Tough Times. https://ie.reachout.com/inform-yourself/family-and-friends/friendships/what-is-friendship/. Accessed on November 9, 2018.

Rosenau, Douglas. A Celebration of Sex: A Guide to Enjoying God's Gift of Married Sexual Pleasure. Nashville: Thomas Nelson, 1994.

Smalley, Gary and Norma Smalley. 4 Days to a Forever Marriage: Choosing Love or Anger. Green Forest, AR: New Leaf Publishing, 2011.

Smalley, Gary. Making Love Last Forever. Dallas: Word Publishing, 1996.

Stanley, Scott, et al. A Lasting Promise: A Christian Guide to Fighting for Your Marriage. San Francisco: Jossey-Bass, 1998.

Stanley, Scott M. The Power of Commitment. San Francisco: Jossey-Bass, 2005.

Tanakh. Hebrew-English Tanakh, Jewish Publication Society. The Traditional Hebrew Text and the New JPS Translation, Second Edition, 1999.

Tannen, Deborah. I Only Say This Because I Love You: How the Way We Talk Can Make or Break Family Relationships. New York: Random House, 2001.

Tannen, Deborah. You Just Don't Understand: Women and Men in Conversation. New York: Ballantine Books, 1990.

Townsend, John. Hiding from Love. Grand Rapids: Zondervan, 1996.

Van Epp, John. *How to Avoid Falling in Love with a Jerk*. New York: McGraw Hill, 2007.

Waltke, Bruce K. *The Book of Proverbs, The New International Commentary on the Old Testament*. Grand Rapids: Eerdmans Publishing Company, 2004.

Williams, Roy H. "Husbands Who Cheat." *The Monday Morning Memo*. http://www.mondaymorningmemo.com/newsletters/husbandswho-cheat/.

Wright, H. Norman and Gary J. Oliver. *How to Change Your Spouse (Without Ruining Your Marriage)*. Ann Arbor: Vine Books, 1994.

Youngs, Bettie and Masa Goetz. *Getting Back Together: How to Reconcile with Your Partner—and Make it Last*. Avon, MA: Adams Media, 2006.

ABOUT THE AUTHOR

Dr. Paul Linzey is the Protestant Chapel Pastor at the United States Naval Academy. In a sense, returning to the Blue Side was a matter of coming full circle because he grew up in a Navy family. His father and brother were Navy chaplains, and one of his sons is currently a Navy chaplain. His other two sons are Army officers.

A pastor before going into the Army chaplaincy, Linzey retired in 2015 at the rank of Colonel. His theme scripture is First Thessalonians 2:8, "We loved you so much that we were willing to share with you not only the gospel of God but our lives as well, because you had become so dear to us."

Linzey is an award-winning author who has written articles for religious and military magazines. He was a contributing writer and editor for Life Publisher's Warriors Bible in 2014. Then in 2019 he published a book called WisdomBuilt: Biblical Principles of Marriage. His second book, released in September 2020, is titled Safest Place in Iraq, and focuses on his experience as a military chaplain in Iraq during the war. Many of his devotional articles can be seen at CBN.org's online magazine.

Linzey completed the Bachelor of Arts in Religious Studies at Vanguard University in Costa Mesa, CA. Graduate degrees include the Master of Divinity at Fuller Theological Seminary, the Doctor of Ministry at Gordon-Conwell Theological Seminary, and an MFA in Creative Writing at the University of Tampa. He taught Creative Writing at Southeastern University in Lakeland, Florida for several years, and has been a featured speaker at several writers conferences and workshops. He is an adjunct professor of Practical Ministry at Southeastern University, and a mentor in their Doctor of Ministry program.

Linzey's wife, Linda, has enjoyed a career as a university professor of Literature and the Humanities. She is also an ordained minister.

Several years ago, the Linzeys were invited to Budapest, Hungary, where they co-taught a three-week intensive course at the Hungarian Bible College, and spoke in churches throughout the region. As a chaplain representing U.S. Central Command, Paul led a five-person team that spent a month teaching at the Royal Academy of Islamic Studies in Amman, Jordan, training their military chaplains and cadets. Throughout their adult life, whether serving in a church, the military, or the university, Paul and Linda have been involved in small group ministries, pastoral care, lay leadership training, and marriage/family seminars and retreats.

Paul's personal interests include music, digital photography, movies and theater, sports, and family. He and his wife have three sons who are military officers, ten grandchildren, and a Beagle named Sophie.

You may contact Dr. Linzey using the contact page of his website: paullinzey.com.

 P & L Publishing
& Literary Services

This book was prepared by P&L Publishing & Literary Services

If you want to self-publish your book, you'll find their prices to be reasonable, and their staff to be professional and friendly.

plpubandlit.com

www.ingramcontent.com/pod-product-compliance
Lightning Source LLC
Chambersburg PA
CBHW060750050426
42449CB00008B/1343

This book is a winner!
—Rich Guerra, Superintendent, SoCal Network

WisdomBuilt Biblical Principles of Marriage combines wisdom from the Bible, clinical research, and personal experience to show couples how to build a great marriage, and provides congregational leaders a practical plan for helping couples in their care. The result is an accessible, easy-to-follow format that may be used in a couples class, sermon series, seminar, or retreat. It may also be helpful in counseling or a private conversation.

The chapter on embracing the image of God in the other is itself worth a read of the full text.
—Dr. Zach Tackett, Professor of Historical Theology & Worship

Taking a very practical approach, the author shows the reader what works and what doesn't, what's biblical and what isn't, what makes sense and what doesn't. Because it draws from the three sources of wisdom, it is part Bible study, part counseling, and part storytelling. Easy to read and follow, readers will find it to be the most interesting and helpful book on marriage they've ever seen.

- Discussion starters after each chapter
- Scriptures for each principle
- Practical examples from real life
- The best of current marriage research
- Invitation to interact with the author
  Contact him at http://paullinzey.com

Paul and Linda Linzey saved our marriage.
—Sig & Becky Fertig, Board of Deacons, Lay Ministry Leaders

Dr. Paul Linzey is a former pastor, military chaplain, and college professor. He and his wife, Dr. Linda Linzey, have conducted marriage seminars and retreats for many years. They are available to speak on marriage and family issues, mentoring, and leadership training at churches, universities, and other groups. They specialize in lay ministry development, and speak to groups of all sizes.

ISBN 9781945976148